NURSE WOLF & DR SACKS

NURSE WOLF & DR SACKS

PAUL THEROUX

 SHORT BOOKS

FRONT LINES

First published in 2001 by
Short Books
15 Highbury Terrace
London N5 1UP

Copyright ©
Paul Theroux 2001

A CIP catalogue record for this book
is available from the British Library.

ISBN 0 571 20840 1

Printed in Great Britain by
Bookmarque Ltd, Croydon, Surrey

To 'Nurse Wolf' and Oliver Sacks,
whose friendship and truthfulness
made this book possible

Photograph: 'Dominatrix', Helmut Newton

NURSE WOLF

The man she called 'the bug cruncher' used to show up at her studio furtively carrying old cloudy Tupperware containers labelled with strips of masking tape scrawled Lasagna April 97 or Spaghetti Sauce. Never mind the labels – the Tupperware contained insects the man had carefully caught in Long Island, where he was a construction worker. He started with beetles, and then he brought roaches and slugs. As time passed the creatures got bigger. One day he brought a live mouse.

Nurse Wolf said to him, 'I draw the line there. I never said I'd do a mouse.'

'Do the mouse,' the man pleaded. 'It's half-dead anyway.' Because it had been in the Tupperware container with no breathing holes.

'I'm like "No way!"' Nurse Wolf told me. But she agreed to do the others. 'I had to wear shoes. He was very specific. Open-toed mules with these high heels.'

The man lay on his side, on the floor – 'the bug's-

7

eye view,' in Nurse Wolf's phrase – tumescent, touching himself.

'Stab it with your heel slowly. He wanted Nurse Wolf to tease and torment the creatures. Then he would say suddenly, 'Crush it!' and clutch himself.

The bug cruncher's fetish was unusual, even in Nurse Wolf's wide experience. And it was difficult for her to squash insects by aiming a stiletto heel at them – they kept slipping, and the slugs were just impossible.

'I liked the freaky side of it,' she said, yet she was soft-hearted towards all creatures. She collected stuffed animals, she loved having pets, she owned a large collection of animal skulls. She had an oryx skull, a giraffe skull and a stuffed beaver she called 'Hoover' in her studio, which she sometimes called her dungeon.

***

Her psychotherapist remained thoughtful when Nurse Wolf told her how, as a dominatrix, she sometimes imagined herself a furry creature with sharp little teeth. When Nurse Wolf added, 'And with a long tail, I have a major tail fetish, I wish I had a tail, I used to wear a tail,' the therapist said, 'That could be penis envy.'

'I have a penis!' Nurse Wolf shouted at her, and she began laughing. 'I have lots of them! I have a long purple one with glitter on it. I have big ones and small ones.

Some are electric. Why should I be envious?'

Some time later Nurse Wolf said to me, 'I love women with tails.'

She also told me, 'I love little fat Hispanic boys with breasts. I have an ass fetish. I can't describe the perfect one but I know it when I see it. I love old men, I love big fat soft men. A few of the fattest and oldest men are my babies. I put diapers on them. I like the ones that just lie there and love the smell of talc, I love the rotten ones too, the ones that are naughty and have to be spanked very hard. Other babies need treatment. I say, "Mommy wants to take your temperature. This is good for you. This is part of your treatment. I'll make this as comfortable for you as possible." I use a dildo, or I might use my finger. If it's my finger I wear gloves, two gloves, one over the other. For fisting I use long-sleeved autopsy gloves that a doctor friend gave me. They're totally great gloves.'

In the world turned upside-down, people in search of pain are nearly as common as people seeking relief from it. This is the other side of treatment. Nurse Wolf was my name for this Queen of Algolagnia – pleasure from pain. She gave pleasure by inflicting it, she got pleasure from causing it. 'Nurse Wolf' because in our talks she described one of her most frequent roles as a nurse in a medical scenario, and it suited her perfectly. I could see the white shoes, the white nurse's outfit, the brisk gestures, the busy hands. In her early thirties, attractive, the picture of health, still looking more like a Texas cheerleader than an art-student – she had been both – it was easy to see her as the efficient and unflappable nurse.

She often referred to skills and actual medical knowledge. In her studio she had a medical room and a lot of implements: tongs and scalpels and electrical devices. I remarked several times on her expertise, her specific operations which she mentioned, for it cannot be easy to sew buttons on a man's skin, or to stitch his penis to his thigh or to put in sutures (even given a dominatrix's skill in tying knots) or to use the sharpest scalpels in the sort of manner that people in her line of work call 'blood play'. But she rejected my compliments and dismissed such procedures as fairly simple – her modest dismissal was very nurse-like – shaking her head and saying, 'It's only home surgery.'

'Typically, I'm an evil nurse,' she explained.

The ritual and theatrical aspects of sexuality were subjects I often pursued with the neurologist Oliver Sacks. He told me how sadistic attacks on plants was for some men a sexual ritual. He also said, 'The universals of costume and uniform become heightened and ritualised in fetishism. Posture is very important. One shows one's posture in one's dress.'

In her wardrobe, which included a French maid's outfit

and the black leather of her biker babe roles – and much else – Nurse Wolf also had the white dress, the hat, the shoes. And then she reflected on the eroticism in finding dramatic uses in her nurse-scenario for rectal thermometers and high colonics and the simple exposures and insertions in the more provocative aspects of prostate-poking – sex as proctology.

'"This is for your own good," I might say. Or it's an examination: "You have to bend over and we have to see if you're worthy to be my slave." With the cross-dressers it's, "Are you a virgin?" It can be a slave-auction scenario, or sheer humiliation. There's something incredibly humiliating and exciting about someone they're overpowered by, and being penetrated by.'

'So you're a wicked nurse?' I asked.

'There's always that wicked side but the question is: how pronounced is it? "Mommy wants to take your temperature." Nurse does that too. It's the same kind of line. "This is part of your treatment." I am more or less in control that way.'

Her authority and assertiveness in the role-playing with her clients derived from the discussion beforehand in which all the options were considered. 'I say, "Paint me an image if you don't know the words for it," and they go, "I used to watch this show and this woman used to wear..." and they describe it. Lots of people love cat-suits. They love Cat Woman in *Batman*. And they love that woman Emma Peel from *The Avengers*.'

If the role-play was nurse–patient, she explained, she would urge the client to recount his history: had he had an experience of nurses or hospitals, or physical examinations, and what about a childhood illness?

The promise of 'authentic medical exam room' is often made in the advertisements for mistresses in the S&M press. Nurse Wolf's medical room was well fitted-out and, with the possible exception of the handcuffs and whips, would not have disgraced a professional gynaecologist's examining room, which it greatly resembled. And there was much more equipment elsewhere in the place. Usually she called it her studio, but sometimes it was 'my dungeon'. Dungeon seemed fairly apt for two of the rooms, given the furnishings: a black coffin, a steel cage, flogging posts and flogging stools, a rubber body bag that was winched up so that a man could hang like a bat. I had never seen so many clothes or such equipment.

'You wouldn't believe my overheads,' Nurse Wolf said.

After many lengthy conversations I seriously wondered whether there was anyone whom Nurse Wolf did not welcome to her place.

Her answer surprised me.

'If someone calls on the phone and says, "I'm very attractive. I work out all the time and make a lot of money" – I have no interest,' Nurse Wolf said. 'And younger men are no good. They think they're so handsome. They don't show up on time. They're not respectful – I don't like the young guys at all. Those "You're-going-to-tie-me-up-and-keep-me-forever" guys.

'What I want to hear is: "I haven't had an extensive amount of real experience, but I want to grow in this area, and I fantasise about X, Y and Z." Maybe they don't know what it means in their life – that it has a place. I have a lot of great clients.'

'What makes a great client?'

'They have a good sense of humour,' she said. 'They respect your time. They like the same things as I do. They trust me and appreciate it. I like grateful and really respectful people. The only downside is that after you beat the hell out of them they call you 20 times afterwards to thank you.'

As with any other treatment centre, a person was not accepted by Nurse Wolf as a client without being first screened and pre-interviewed, and there was always the question of money. She charged $200 an hour for clients of long-standing, $250 for newer clients, sometimes more for lengthy sessions. 'I love the crazies and the psycho people – but they are so unstable.'

'I imagine flogging someone is pretty exhausting, isn't it? How many would you do in a day?'

'Not many. But I might do longer sessions.'

'What's a long session?'

'The longest I like to do is ten hours.'

Which was $2,000, but as Nurse Wolf quickly pointed out it required considerable preparation and a lot of cleaning up afterwards. 'This business can be profitable. Some people make it very profitable. But I travel so much. Also I am selective. I don't see it as a business as much as I should. Another mistress would have other people working. Or would not have so much equipment. They would try to keep their overheads lower. I don't want to do that. I know people who have 900 lines and websites. They offer videos and phone sessions.'

Screening was essential. Walk-ins were out of the question; no drop-ins, no strangers. Even men Nurse Wolf thought she knew well had become stalkers, and there were non-stop phone freaks. She knew that when she was alone with her clients anything could happen. The previous summer a dominatrix on the Upper West Side had been found bludgeoned to death in her dungeon.

'I am worried about that,' Nurse Wolf said. 'The clients know where you are and they think they have something over your head.'

One of Nurse Wolf's objections to working in a house – as she did early in her career – was that the clients were not properly screened. Some men wanted sessions with her but considered her unclean, wanted her to cover herself completely in transparent plastic wrap, or others implored her to strip, 'which was out of the question'. And others did not want to be dominated at all. 'One guy stuck my head in a toilet. I had no idea that I was expected to be a slave at times. I had limits. And, of course, in a house they want you to do volume.'

So, as Nurse Wolf, and sometimes Mistress Wolf, or Mommy, she screened everyone beforehand. 'I have them write letters. There are a number of things they have to do for me. They have to draw a portrait of themselves on the outside of the envelope, and they also have to include a picture of their pet, or someone else's pet – choosing a pet picture tells me a lot about a person. What they're like, their sense of humour. A lot.'

After that she talked to the prospective clients on the phone. And when they arrived for their session there was more preparation – discussion, perhaps an hour or more of it, before the session started.

I asked, 'If I said, "Would you see my friend?" would you?'

'I would want to know a lot – whether the friendship was personal or professional. I'd ask what sort of experience he's had: "Who have you really enjoyed seeing?" If someone says, "No one"– a first-timer – I'm not going to see them, because I'm not sure what I am going to find.'

She was one of the busiest and most successful mistresses in Manhattan. As for the preferences, there were all sorts, but there was a certain random synchronicity to her clients' demands that developed day by day.

'It goes in waves. I don't know how it happens – it's like being in the subway and everyone's chosen to wear green. One day will be all sissy-maid-cross-dressers-slut-day. And the next day very heavy leather.'

**

We met, she and I, as travellers, just by chance, both of us being cagey about what we really did for a living, like a bishop and an actress thrown together on the Amazon. She said she was a photographer, I mumbled something about journalism. In fact I was working on a novel and she was travelling with one of her slaves, whom she buggered every morning and beat every night – though I was never privileged to observe this unusual spectacle (unusual, at least, in the mellow monotony of a jungle setting).

She said she travelled extensively, and it had to be true, for she was knowledgeable and confident. But it was only long after, when we came clean about how we were both self-employed ('I have a dungeon;' 'I'm a novelist') that she told me how she travels with some clients, prosperous businessmen, heads of companies, tying them up and whipping them back at the hotel after all the day's meetings are over. She travelled abroad – with a bias for Germany and Holland and England. She liked all her clients but she had a special fondness for the English ones.

'They have a cutely developed sense of kink. They love games. They're also very polite – respectful and formal. And they can be real sluts,' she said, smiling with genuine approval. Her descriptive language interested me, because it did not come out of books – she had read almost nothing and yet she sometimes used the neurological or psychological phrases that Oliver Sacks used. For example, speaking of the English she said, 'What matters more is that it's all about some structure and ritual.'

I took to her and she to me. 'We both have "people skills",' I said. She laughed at that. She laughed a lot – I liked her cheery mood.

'Hey, I'm busy, I've things to do and people to beat!' she said sometimes.

Or: 'Come on over and let's see what we can whip up.' Some were the well-honed ripostes of a professional pleaser, but most was the good humour a person derives from sheer fulfilment. I saw my Doctor Lauren Slaughter, resident of Half-Moon Street – daytime post-graduate student and night-time 'escort' – as the embodiment of much of the ambition and self-delusion of the 1980s. Nurse Wolf I saw as a Doctor Slaughter for the 1990s – not just servicing flagellomaniacs but with a cultural perspective. She really was a photographer, a record-cover designer and maker of videos; she liked the movie *Crumb* and all sorts of performance art. She had an enthusiastic appreciation of modern art. Talking about Francis Bacon one day I mentioned that he was a masochist who was whipped every evening by his cockney lover ('Ready for yer frashing now, Frawncis?'), and she gushed, 'I love his paintings. I would love to have whipped Francis Bacon.' Pop music, even if it wasn't mainstream, was a passion. She knew everything about rock groups like 'Nashville Pussy' or acts such as the 'Pain-Proof Rubber Girls'. There were two Rubber Girls. They contorted together in erotic postures on a bed of nails. They also put cigarettes out on their tongues.

After telling me how people did something shocking like that Nurse Wolf would say, 'Maybe they don't do it in your world but they do in mine.' I liked that very much, her referring to my world and her world.

Her world I knew from advertisements in magazines. It has never been hard to figure out the personal ads; indeed they have become less entertaining as they have grown more specific. 'Cute Jewish male, 55. Very fit, own business seeks full-figured Jewish female 22-35 for travel southern CA coast' is not necessarily about marriage, whereas 'Marriage-minded Catholic female, 34, seeks smart, fun, white successful professional NYC male who has never been married' certainly is. The more upbeat such ads sound the more desperate they seem, but the subtext of loneliness and frustration is obviously part of the attraction.

Alongside such ads there is another sort of classification that, until recently, I had found pretty hard to decode. For decades 'massage' and 'relaxation therapy' have been euphemisms for masturbation, but the category of 'Role Play' in mainstream weekly magazines I found distinctly peculiar. The wording of a typical ad, 'Sultry Diva – Let me train you... Now! – Fetish Exploration/Behaviour Modification/Nurse Therapy,' just baffled me.

Role-playing was one of Nurse Wolf's specialities. And in a profession where talk costs money and the meter is always running, Nurse Wolf was easy-going and talkative. Her garrulity appealed to me because she was so candid. And her work was not just a job. She was clearly sexually obsessed. Her role-playing was less a living than a way of life that she had been refining since puberty.

She had grown up in a middle-class home, in a suburb, by a swimming pool, in an indulgent family, and was still in regular touch with her folks (Once, her father called her on her cellular phone while I was in her dungeon: 'I'm talking to Paul Theroux... the writer... yeah, I'll tell him you like his stuff.') She was educated in private schools; she had gone to a great art college. Almost more than anything, I was fascinated by her prosperous upbringing, her prep school, her cheerleading. What struck me in her reminiscences were her distinct and detailed memories of her girlhood, her close touch with her sexual memory.

'I have a suspicion that obsessive sexuality goes with a clear, continuous and conscious memory of childhood sexual desire, fantasies and even activity, without the latent period that other people have,' Oliver Sacks had once said to me.

To a novelist, latency is a nuisance and access to the past is a kind of magic – all the better when what is revealed is something forbidden or strange. What I regarded as unspeakable rituals she would term 'play'. Again, a psychologist's term. And I was fascinated by how immediate her history was to her. Perhaps, as Oliver said, it was part of her obsessive sexuality.

***

And then there was the question of her world, which was an actual world, one that more and more was referred to in my world in the algolagnic imagery in fashion ads – the long metal heel of a Gucci shoe (called 'The Stiletto') pressed on to a man's hairy chest. Gucci offers a stylish nipple ring in silver for $895. In an ad for Bass Ale, a man is shown licking a woman's latex boot ('In a world of strange tastes, there's always Bass Ale'). 'Tongue for Rent' is the copy in an ad for a New York wine merchant, and there is predictably pervy imagery in an ad for Fetish perfume. Add to these the allegations of the sexual amusements of a well-known sportscaster waiting in fish-net stockings and a garter belt for his date; and a political adviser in a Washington hotel room with a call-girl who enjoyed (according to the call-girl) being naked on all fours, wearing a dog collar and barking, 'Woof-woof!'

The Robert Mapplethorpe photographic exhibition that travelled across America from 1988 to 1990 was a significant event in publicising the varieties of sexual experience: black leather bullies, men in chains and wear-ing muzzles and leashes, urolagnia, genital mutilation, fisting, clamping, piercing were all lovingly adumbrated, along with the photographer's self-portrait in which he depicted himself with a bullwhip rammed up his bum. Mapplethorpe regarded his show as news and he was satisfied when he achieved his goal of shocking the straight world. Was this inspirational? Perhaps so. It gave at least one Versace fashion show a style – bondage clothes. The work of another photographer, Eric Kroll, is just as bizarre yet in a sense more appealing than Mapplethorpe's – no blood, for one thing. Kroll's photographs of women in bondage, 'Beauty Parade and Fetish Girls', have an allegorical quality though many are also straightforward pornography. Books which would have only been available from speciality bookstores are now mass-market items.

And one night after looking over my Nurse Wolf notes I saw a television comedy, *Just Shoot Me*, in which one of the characters, Dennis Finch (played by David Spade), becomes madly attracted to a fashion model and ends up suspended in her bedroom in a cage – an actual cage, a classic piece of S&M apparatus, with the laugh-line about the willowy fashion model being a closet dominatrix. This gimmick went through various permutations, but the plot-point was insistent in implying that Dennis rather liked the experience and happily went back for more punishment. That was shown at primetime on NBC on a weeknight a few days before Christmas.

Nurse Wolf had just such a cage in her dungeon, which was in an older red-brick building in a busy neighbourhood in Manhattan. It was no more than a numbered door in the middle of a block, the sort of place that is easy to slip into and out of unnoticed.

Up one steep flight to a small landing and another door giving on to a narrow corridor and small rooms leading to the 'studios'. Far from having the atmosphere of a commercial space, it looked like an apartment that has been turned into a series of smaller rooms. I smelled the burning candles, that aroma of chapels and altars, long before I entered the room. There were 30 or more candles burning in the room – from tall dripping candles to vigil lights flickering in cups of liquid wax. They eerily illuminated the room, which would have been eerie even without candle flames. The first object to catch my eye was a steel coffin standing upright with a cross cut in its lid, and what I took to be a table looked like a steel cage.

'Yes, it is a cage,' Nurse Wolf said, 'but it doubles as a table. I use it as a cage, for overnighters.'

Another world, yes, but a recognisable one, for this was clearly a torture chamber. Because of the candle flames, the large room was all jumping shadows and wisps of smut and smoke. Black leather predominated. On a suspended steel carousel there was a selection of black leather whips, 50 or more, all types, from horse crops and long whips to the vicious leather whip I recognised as a South African *sjambok*, the very symbol of apartheid. Dangling from other hooks, there were black leather muzzles, studded black leather masks, and bridles and bits, leather gags, nooses. Nurse Wolf sat on the top of the cage in black leather pants and boots and a white T-shirt. Behind her was a large leather seat I took to be a swing.

'What is the purpose of that swing?'

'Sling,' she said, correcting me. 'Typically in gay culture you'd say it was a "fisting sling". It supports a very vulnerable bondage position where you're completely immobilised. The idea is that you sit on the very edge here. Your legs are shackled and your arms tied. Then you're completely exposed to whatever happens to you.'

'And what might that be?'

'Fisting, but I don't do much fisting any more,' Nurse Wolf said. 'I loved it. It was like stuffing a turkey. It can take an hour to open a guy up, but one guy was a lot easier – more open.

'Or you can do relatively tight bondage in it – which I prefer, honestly. I like it when people don't move at all, or that they can move a little bit but they're still not going anywhere.'

That tight bondage was more a reflection of her own skill, for it was important to Nurse Wolf that the person to be treated felt completely helpless, unable even to wriggle.

'They get into a state of acceptance much more quickly if they're completely immobilised,' she said. 'Or they become completely traumatised. It's one or the other.'

When I asked, 'Do they get more excited the tighter it is?' she said that it was impossible to generalise, and she made a larger and more pedantic point. She was insistent that I refrain from generalising about any part of what she did. 'People are all different,' she said. I misunderstood if I noticed a classical piece of torture apparatus and saw only a person writhing in pain. 'Respecting limits' and 'passing to another level' were both repeated mantras in the world of S & M and role-playing. Cross-dressing did not mean that a man wanted actually to change his gender, for this was role-play: 'If someone's being forced into cross-dressing they don't want necessarily to be a woman, but they want to be treated like a slutty woman and kind of forced to do things that are their worst nightmare, that are also very exciting.'

'Forced cross-dressing' meant that she dressed them. 'I constantly get requests for this kind of thing. Every level of clothing. They say, "I have to be made to do it."' If they enjoyed cross-dressing without needing for it to be demanded of them, they often brought their own wardrobe. Sometimes they arrived soberly dressed in a business suit but underneath wore women's underwear. And any sort of dressing might involve a whipping.

I remarked on the whips – their number, their complexity, the quality, too, for they were well-made.

'Is that a mace?' It was a heavy spiked ball attached by a thick chain to a club. Traditionally, a mace was a war club used to smash body armour.

'I haven't used it yet,' she said. 'Let's see, what else? These are nice. I like these padded muzzles.'

It was another black leather piece, heavily stitched, with fasteners. The strength of the equipment was impressive, but of course this was not merely costume stuff for a musical of *The Man in the Iron Mask* or *Dracula*, or for dressing up for a costume ball; this muzzle was buckled to a man's face and put to the test.

'This one was made to order, because I wanted it to be able to be tied down. I like to do head bondage. I need stuff that you can attach to other things.'

She saw me smiling in bewilderment.

'It's a playground,' she said.

And there were masks on a shelf above the cage. Silly rubber masks, and animal masks, and hoods. One which even Nurse Wolf agreed was particularly scary was a hood mask with no eye holes, padded ears to muffle sound, with only a small breathing hole at the mouth.

'It's got headphones in here at the ears so they're completely disoriented. It's scary. You can try it on if you want. It's really claustrophobic.'

I said no. I changed the subject to the huge steel coffin that stood upright dominating the rear of the dungeon.

'A friend of mine is a sculptor. He made it for me. I watched a lot of Hammer movies when I was a kid, so this is totally my fetish, you know? I use it very infrequently here, unless I'm playing with someone who's really crazy about it.'

'Have you been in it?'

'Yes. I like it. Get into it so that you can hear what it sounds like.'

I got into the coffin. Nurse Wolf closed the lid. I felt the sensation of being buried alive: I was squeezed and suffocated and plunged into a soundless blackness. I felt for a way of freeing myself but I touched only a series of hooks around the edge, which were for restraining the coffin occupant.

'Isn't that coffin totally great?' Nurse Wolf said through the small cut-out cross in the lid.

***

Another day, feeling that I knew only her professional life, I asked her to reconstruct the previous 24 hours. I was interested in what a typical day might be, including free time and domestic activity. I was now well aware that she whipped men for a living – and not only whipped them but indulged them in all sorts of ways, from listening to their bizarre fantasies to suspending them from the ceiling in rubber body-bags. And there were also the diapers and the sutures.

I had wondered: does she do it just for the money or is she compulsive? The answer was, thunderously, that she was compulsive – that thought and fantasy and dedication were all part of her effort; she found what she did exhausting but also vastly enjoyable. She liked her clients – liked them best when they were wordlessly being flogged. The ones she did not like she sent away, and she regarded her refusal to whip them as the worst punishment she could inflict on them.

The previous day had been Sunday. Sundays in the straight world tend to be different from weekdays, but her Sunday – this one at any rate – she said was an average day, except that she had had trouble with her car.

The day had started all right, though. 'I woke up at seven or eight and made seared tuna with this wasabi-soy marinade. I have fish every morning for breakfast. Then I left at about 12 and helped my boyfriend with his computer for a little while.'

So far, apart from the wasabi-soy marinade, this seemed the sort of unexceptional Sunday anyone might have. But it was still only noon.

'I had a session around one,' Nurse Wolf said. 'I was a little late. He drove in – it's an hour or so – from Queens. When he saw I hadn't arrived he called me on my cellular phone. I told him to go buy some seltzer water. They're always happier if they have some little tasks. Then he arrives and says, "Nice pants". They were new, beautiful tiger-stripe pants. I decided to be nice to him. We talked for a little while. Then I tormented him. I gave him some heavy nipple stuff – really squeezed his nipples. He wasn't tied up. He was still dressed, which is more of a trauma. I tied him up – face up. Very few are face down. If they're face up there's more to play with.'

Casting her mind back to her narrative of the previous day she frowned, and hesitated, and shook her head. I sensed a certain regret in the set of her mouth.

'I decided to try something new,' she said. She sighed. That was obviously the regret. 'I thought it would be great, but no – it was a mistake. I had to fuck with the perfect mixture. I could have just let him suck my dirty toes. If I had just come from the gym I could have let him lick my armpits. I had forgotten that he didn't like anything anal. But I stuck my finger in him – I was wearing several gloves – and I could tell he was disappointed. He didn't really like it. I love piercing and probing. Here's a body. You can probe it. But he didn't have a great reaction to it. After the session he says, "It's really uncomfortable. It's really weird. Maybe it's the way I'm built."'

The man then left, unsatisfied, perhaps disturbed – emotions which Nurse Wolf shared, for she had hoped to bring him to another level, and it had failed. Such men were usually predictable, she said – not like babies in her infantilism role-playing. She should have stuck with the man's own requirements, cliché-ridden as they might have seemed.

As though jinxed she left her dungeon and had trouble with her car. The key wouldn't turn in the door lock. 'I couldn't get my finger into his ass, couldn't get the key into the lock. I didn't push any of the right buttons!

It's Sunday – no mechanic. I went to K-Mart for some WD-40.'

I tried to imagine Nurse Wolf shopping in big biker boots, with her big leather backpack on Aisle 9 ('Automotive') – Attention K-Mart shoppers! – looking for heavy-duty motor lubricants. But there were probably others dressed just like her on this New York Sunday.

The WD-40 didn't work. She fussed with the car lock for a while, then around six went back to the dungeon to change for dinner. She then got a call from a mistress friend, Dale, inviting her over to her place to drop in on a session in progress.

'I've got a dinner engagement. I can give you 40 minutes,' Nurse Wolf said.

The client turned out to be a mystery. Neither Dale nor Nurse Wolf had ever seen his face. 'He always comes in a business suit, wearing a latex cat suit under it, and that includes a mask,' she told me. 'It's custom-made. He wears dark glasses, too. From the look of his body he's in his mid to late 30s. He's in good shape. It makes me think that he might be famous or recognisable. You never know. He might just be paranoid.'

I said, 'If Dale doesn't know his name, what does she call him?'

' "Slave", "Cock-sucker". She calls him a lot of things.'

It was early evening, seven o'clock, by the time Nurse

Wolf had dressed and put on her make-up. She went in wearing what the man had requested – a cat-suit and thigh-high boots. The man's head and feet were tied down, but his hands and arms were free.

Dale was sitting on a throne behind his head, with her feet on his chest.

Nurse Wolf said, 'Why are this pathetic creature's hands not tied?'

'Oh, because even though he's doing a horrible job I'm trying to teach him to worship my legs.'

'Isn't this a waste of your valuable time?'

'I don't know why I bother!' And Dale said to the man, 'You don't know how lucky you are. I can't believe she'd be interested in seeing someone like you – she is Mistress Wolf. And you can't even massage my feet well.'

'Does he do anything right?' Nurse Wolf said.

'Hardly,' Dale said, stepping on the man's face.

The two women started to laugh. The man made 'barnyard sounds' inside his hood. He was tied face up with chains between two posts on the floor. His hands were free but his penis and testicles were tied with surgical tubing to his toes. Dale got up from her throne and they started to do a dance over him.

The exciting part of a session, Nurse Wolf said, was not quite knowing where it was leading – extemporising, in the manner of method actors preparing a scene. So the women danced on the hooded man. Readers of *Vogue*, *Elle* and *Harper's Bazaar* will find what followed vividly familiar, for the dominatrices' sharp heels pierced the man's chest as clearly depicted in the Gucci ad for their popular shoe The Stiletto.

Dale said, 'I think I have to pee.'

Nurse Wolf said, 'Well, I really have to go, so I'll do that part if you want – but I don't want him to see.'

The man was berated into putting his hands over the holes in his hood, while Nurse Wolf squatted and urinated on Dale's toes. 'I'd never done that before. It was so great I loved it. I couldn't care less about men. This is so much not for men.' Dale put her feet in his mouth and demanded that he suck her toes. The man hesitated and seemed to panic.

'I'm afraid I'll do it wrong,' the hooded man wailed

'Like everything else you do,' Dale said, and the women laughed again. 'What a wuss you are!'

The man was confused; tied up, writhing, he struggled to think of the right answer, while the two women stood upon his naked body.

I wondered aloud whether he had liked his session.

'They always do when you're enjoying yourself,' Nurse Wolf said.

She did not speculate on who the man might be. 'I'm not really up on who people are, but someone would probably recognise him.' She did not ask: she respected a person's demands and she wanted hers to be respected. It was important in such a business for people to be comfortable, and – paradoxically, given the fact that they were flogged unmercifully – to feel safe.

The session ended. Nurse Wolf changed her clothes again, met her boyfriend and they went out to eat at a good restaurant with another couple and enjoyed an excellent meal.

All in all, Nurse Wolf thought, not a bad day.

***

'I didn't start out wanting to be a professional mistress at all,' Nurse Wolf said. It had started purely as play, in her prep school. In the seventh grade, at age 13, she had become a cheerleader for the school team. Homecoming was a big Texas thing, lasting a whole week. It involved the whole school. One of the festivities was a slave auction.

'You could buy anyone that day,' Nurse Wolf said. 'I forget what the other days were. Obviously for me Slave Day was a little more prominent than all the other days. You could buy a slave for the week. Anybody could buy anybody, and there were groups of people that would buy someone.'

This voluntary slave auction was for a charity; for the Pep Club, or whatever the current campaign might be –

hunger or homelessness. The stipulation was that within limits it was acknowledged as public humiliation. 'It was flattering to be bought and it was also a horrible thing,' Nurse Wolf said. 'Seventh grade was the year I bought Kent Sanford. I'd had a crush on him for years. Finally I bought him and he was mine. I dressed him in my cheerleading outfit, with full make-up, and that's how it all started.' Kent loved it. Nurse Wolf realised that Kent had perhaps never cross-dressed before that. He was transformed – he fell utterly for Nurse Wolf.

The next year, when she was in the eighth grade, the television series *Roots* came out. The dynamics of the master–slave relationship and the details of domination and submission – the whips, the handcuffs, the shouted orders, the pleading – had a profound effect on her. She saw every episode of *Roots*. She began to think that you could make anyone do anything.

'My mother used to say, "Men and boys only tease you when they like you." Basically I guess I was fascinated by what I could make them do just by telling them. They would do the silliest things. They didn't want to make decisions. They wanted a girl to say, "Wear my underwear!"'

The notions came through play and experiment. And she admitted that at first she had no clear idea what she was doing, that she was travelling down a road that was first surveyed by the Marquis de Sade. She never read anything about it. Reading did not feature much in shaping or informing her in her tastes. ('You know Krafft-Ebing's notorious study *Psychopathia Sexualis*?' I asked her once and she said, 'Who?') Her tastes were shaped in the time-honoured way: learning by doing.

'They said, "Do I have to?" I said, "Of course you have to. I won you in an auction!"'

She had a series of 'semi-platonic' boyfriends after that. There was no sex but there was serious play. 'In Texas you get all this pool activity. I would draw on them with lipstick and then send them home. They'd worry that their mother or their maids would find out. It was tricky for them.'

None of them objected – at least none of the boys she met. She was being playful. The play continued into high school. Her choice of college was fairly easy. She liked art and design. She was a serious student but was also simultaneously broadening her interests in S & M. She had friends at nearby colleges. 'I used to play with them and used to photograph their heavy scenes. They were into a lot of blood play.'

After graduation in the mid-1980s she came to New York. The S & M scene was less open; people met at parties – 'play parties'. 'I dressed. I was a sadist. But you don't learn the skills overnight.'

The play at parties seldom went on in private rooms, and the public nature of these displays of domination and submission meant that a practitioner could quite quickly develop a reputation for being an expert mistress. Nurse Wolf was observed and admired; she was invited to work at various dungeons. The first was the now-defunct West-Side Dungeon, which was run by a Hasidic man.

Nurse Wolf said that 15 years ago there had been far fewer establishments in New York than there were now. Even she was astonished by how popular such activity was, how accessible, how much of its imagery in the mainstream. Still, she was less surprised by the clients than the mistresses in the houses.

'Some of those people I wouldn't let out on the street. The mistresses were psychotic. And I had more equipment at home than they had in their studios. They'd have a piece of rope and a Ping-Pong paddle. I had beautiful custom-made leather whips.'

She had to lay down ground rules: No 'toilet service'. No foul name-calling. Hasidic men could be trying. 'They find women filthy. They want everything to be kosher in a way – "Is everything safe? Is everything clean?" Then it's, "Can you beat me on the hands and tell me I'm bad?" They think I'm unclean. They are really into the visual. So it's, "Take your blouse off." There's no way I would do that. I am not going to undress for them. This young kid

36

says to me, "Let's see what you have between your legs," which I find offensive. I said, "I have a raw piece of pork between my legs."'

One day she was asked to do a Hasidic man who smelled terrible. He had not washed. He demanded 'a Nazi interrogation' in which she was to be the Bitch of Buchenwald, questioning him, slapping his face, abusing him verbally. He gave her precise instructions: she was to wear shiny black boots and a cap with a shiny black visor, and black leather gloves.

She had been warned about this man but she knew him by another name. She was too new to the business to know that clients visiting houses had many aliases. This was an unstable man.

He was tied up but his head was not tied, and at the end of the session, thoroughly interrogated and humiliated, he kissed her when she leaned too close, sticking his tongue in her mouth. That earned him the hardest slap of the session. Nurse Wolf was angry and disgusted – she hurried away and gargled with peroxide. And afterwards the man took a shower.

'That pissed me off. Not before, but after he had been with me. See?'

In all her stories of whippings and cutting and broken canes and blood, few things offended her more than that unwelcome kiss. Speaking of the risks in her work, she told me about it more than once, always in tones of amazement and disgust.

'So there are some things that repel you?'

'Yes, but mainly I don't want to be told what to do.'

The technical term for this kind of client is SAMs – Smart-Ass Masochists, or 'Topping from the Bottom' – a slave giving orders. Nurse Wolf described it as back-seat driving, and hated it.

'And there are things you like to do?'

'Oh yes. I love everything I do, or else I wouldn't do it.'

There was such intensity in the way Nurse Wolf spoke about her fantasies and her own pleasure that the word 'work' was inadequate for what she did every day. I found her funny, friendly and generous. She was knowledgeable about painting, photography, and pop music and performance art. She had a wide circle of friends. She was widely travelled. And, as she worked out in a gym most days, she was in superb physical condition: in our usual farewell bear-hug she unfailingly left me winded.

But by almost any reckoning she was involved in the darkest pleasures imaginable. She described many of them to me in detail, down to the exhausted howls of pleasure of a manacled and bent-over man, his skin splitting open and blood bursting from it under the crack of a whip. 'The chance to probe someone's body,' as she put it, gave her intense pleasure. She was fascinated by Japanese rope

38

bondage and esoteric knots, by any variation that fed her sadism. 'Very subtle changes make me very happy.'

But what was the point of all this pain and darkness? Nurse Wolf said, 'Hot things to me are not dark.' A look of pleasurable anticipation that brought to mind a sharp appetite lighted her face whenever an image of submission was suggested. 'Girls look great when they're tied up,' she said. 'Some men take me girlfriends as a sort of offering.' But Nurse Wolf was so ambiguous sexually that words such as gay or straight do not begin to describe the nuances of her polymorphous perversity, nor her quest for erotic variation which makes *The Story of O* seem like a simple prologue to her pleasures.

There was a man who impressed her by having the highest pain threshold she had ever encountered. 'I broke canes on him,' she said admiringly. And there was the cross-dressing college friend, whom she described to me as 'a rat boy sheltering in the comfort of other men'.

There were people who would see her for a session every day if she agreed.

But shaking her head she admitted the paradox: 'These people are junkies.'

'I am looking for a man who can take anything,' she told me. 'I have found one, but not a sane one, just the crazies.' With one man, a successful businessman and obsessive masochist, it was almost love. He could take anything. He kept asking for more. 'I pushed him to another level, and then I couldn't handle it. It was the pain. I don't think he had ever been beaten as hard as I was beating him. And then he was craving it. He was into services – being tied up and played with. I ran him through the wringer. He had to work for everything. And because I was attracted to him, I was beating him harder each time. Usually on the ass. After a caning I don't think he could undress in front of his wife for weeks. I would break canes on him, too.'

The man ceased to be a client, left his wife, became Nurse Wolf's lover – well, a sort of lover: her utter slave. But his almost limitless capacity for degradation became such a burden it was as though she was his servant, and at last he exhausted her patience. 'I don't think I'd ever do anything like that again. It was awful.'

This talk of variety led inevitably to her wondering where my pleasure lay.

'I think I am pretty dull,' I said. This talk of pain did nothing but turn my manhood into a peanut.

'No one's dull.'

'Maybe,' I said. 'Funnily enough, the brand-name Rubbermaid has always interested me for some reason.'

'Yeah.' And she smiled wickedly, looking into my heart. She said, 'I like Rubber Queen!'

At the house she worked in shifts, of five to seven

hours, getting $70 out of the $200 the client paid. She sometimes did 12-hour sessions.

But she left the house. 'I didn't want to be chosen from a book. One time I had a handprint on my face from a slap. I ended a great relationship over that.'

Off and on she worked in houses for five years. The best place she worked was 'The Nut-Cracker Suite', which is still in business. In a house she was on call, she had to see everyone. She liked the freedom of just coming and going, but there were problems if she broke the rules; and there were penalties, a fine for each infraction. She was fined for being late, fined for running over a session. In a dungeon, more than in most businesses, time was money.

Regular work in houses had allowed Nurse Wolf to accumulate some savings. Using that she set up on her own. To someone unfamiliar with the world of S & M it may seem unusual that a plumber or electrician would arrange a sort of barter in return for his work, but this was the case for some sub-contractors, whose tastes were masochistic. After a day's work putting a ballcock in the toilet or replacing the washers in the medical room faucets, the plumber stripped naked, and Nurse Wolf bent him over her flogging stool and thrashed the daylights out of him.

This subject came up when I speculated about the wealth of her clients. Most were powerful men, but some had very little money, or had been laid off; and some people saved up for a long time to pay for a session. Nurse Wolf said that she often reduced her rates or played with them in return for work they might do at her studio.

'There's an electrician. He's been laid off his job. He'll come in and do things. And I have people who come in and clean. I do sessions with them if they can't afford it.'

'So an electrician or a cleaner will say, "I'm into forcible cross-dressing."'

'It will be something that I suggest. And it will only be after I've known them for a while.'

'What will you suggest?'

She pursed her pretty lips in reflection, then said, 'I needed some errands done. I didn't want them to be done by someone who wanted to be a houseboy or a slave. I wanted it to be by someone I trusted, who knew my real name, my bank account, when I sent out chunks of money to pay things. Someone who could clean a little and that didn't act so slavey that I didn't want him around. So I found someone and I asked if he wanted to do things every week or couple of weeks in return for a session. He was delighted.'

'What did he like?'

'Very heavy corporal things. So I could cane him as hard as I liked. He liked being passed around to friends. He was grateful for every bit of attention.'

'Where would he normally be caned? On the ass?'

'Uh-huh. But he could take it anywhere. I just don't want to injure someone. I do it on the back. The soles of the feet are fine. But I've seen people bullwhipped and it wraps around the calf or their chest and I think it's dangerous.'

Nurse Wolf was not unusual in finding mechanics or housekeepers who would work for a whipping. In the domination newspapers, *S&M News*, *Dominant View* and *Dominant Mystique*, there were often classifieds suggesting whippings for work. 'Young, attractive & Very Experienced Dominant Female with Complete Dungeon, seeks Dedicated Submissive Male Carpenter... to Make Fairly Sophisticated Dungeon Furniture and do alterations to my home in exchange for time spent as your personal temptress, torturer, and object of all your submission.'

Nurse Wolf's dungeon was expensive for her to set up, but operating on her own was preferable to being a mistress in a house or large dungeon.

For one thing it was more profitable, but more than anything she began to understand that repeat business was the best, most dependable, and the safest. Clients from the houses followed her to her studio the way patients follow a dental hygienist who moves to another practice. Some of Nurse Wolf's clients had been seeing her for eight or nine years, others she had known even longer. 'I've done people before they've met their wives, before they've had kids. Their kids are now growing up.'

A client she had been seeing for seven years had just recently said he had something very important to tell her. He wanted to tell her his real name. It was one of the most dramatic moments in all her dealings with him. Nurse Wolf told him it was not necessary for him to divulge his actual identity, but he insisted.

'For him it was a big thing – that he trusted me enough to tell it to me.'

Nurse Wolf liked such people because she enjoyed working with clients who had very intricate fantasies that became more complex over time and demanded intense role-playing, such as the man whose role-playing took place entirely in an office – the scene was probably based on his own office.

'The names of the people are very important in this office,' Nurse Wolf explained. The cast of characters was large – everyone except this man was female. 'He is the only man who's left in this all-woman company. He has done something wrong. He's wrongfully accused of sneaking a glance at a woman – he's presented with an ultimatum, about losing his job, not for making an obscene gesture but for this glance. It's dress-down day. A complaint is filed. It's all women. They say, "No man should be allowed to do this." He has a choice – get fired and lose all his benefits and money and everything, or agree to be a slave.'

'And you beat him?'

'No. He's not tied up – we sit here talking. He's forced to make a decision about being completely destitute, or to have a contract with the office to live there – to live there naked, to be like a toilet servant.

'We've now designed a cage for him in one fantasy. It's got a thing that he drinks out of, much like a hamster would – all the toilets feed into that. He licks my toilet. After I've cleaned it. I know he would lick it no matter what, but I don't want him to lick something that's filthy. I don't want people to lick the bottom of my shoes. I know they would. But I don't want them to get some wacky disease.'

Among her most devoted clients were the ones she called her babies. Speaking of baby culture, the role-playing called infantilism, Nurse Wolf became almost sentimental. In her smirking, sadistic heart there was something strongly maternal. It was her passion for control, her love of detail, and her particular liking for passive clients and unexpected mischief. Babies satisfied her on many levels.

'My fat old babies,' Nurse Wolf said, smiling at the thought.

'They're so cute. I used to see more than I do now, but

I've disassembled my nursery. It's so jammed with stuff. I need more closet space!'

She used to have a playpen – a big one, with steel bars. She even had a baby, Bambi, a grown woman ('She'd scare a real baby terribly') who played at infantilism. 'Bambi and I met at the Babyland photo shoot. She wanted a full-time mommy and I wanted a full-time baby. She was a rotten baby. She got spanked a lot. I didn't have to change her diapers – she wasn't into that. She did things in order to be punished. Which I like. I like that kind of rotten baby. I also like the sweet ones that just lie there.'

For babies she wore a French maid or a pink satin mommy outfit. 'I'm cartoon Mommy, with big high shoes and stockings and lips like this,' she said, pursing her lips and making a fish mouth. Babies are more specific about their wardrobe than any other role-playing client.

'Like three – not two, not four – layers of diapers. They have to be cotton. "I want those bunnies with the pencils on them!"'

Some babies would say, 'I want to go on an adventure!' Nurse Wolf, ever obliging, would take them on an adventure. They'd wear diapers and plastic pants under their clothes, making crinkling sounds as they walk.

'I take this one old baby with one of my girlfriends,' Nurse Wolf said. 'She comes and visits me. She's a great mistress. She's wicked. We're in a bar and I say to the baby,

"You stand over there," and we make out – this is in a bar around the corner – and she torments him, blows smoke into his face. The baby poops in his pants. We make him play pool, or stand up and sit down really hard.'

Of all her clients, she said, the babies were the least predictable. It was possible to make generalisations about leather fetishists, flagellomaniacs, blood players, toilet servants, masochists, slaves, sensory-deprivation junkies and even perhaps bug crunchers, but when it came to infantilism anything was possible. Some were interested only in being dressed. Others had to be changed constantly. Some misbehaved in order to be punished.

Others just lay there wanting to be caressed. They loved the smell of talc. Some loved the experience of being diapered, others craved bottle feeding, and you never knew what they wanted in their bottle – beer, chocolate milk, Coke, whatever. Sensual babies wanted to feel safe. Naughty babies tried to get under Nurse Wolf's skirt and had to be restrained. Some babies loved roaming the streets. That baby they took to the pool room wanted to be called, 'Stinky Poo-Poo Pants'.

In their own worlds, the babies were often power-brokers needing to submit; to be caned, to be mommied. These were grown men, big men in every respect – businessmen, heads of companies, stock-analysts, real-estate speculators, corporate attorneys and others, who liked nothing better than engaging for an hour or two a week in Mommy–Baby role-play.

Two generalisations were possible. Baby clients were always shaved. And also, babies loved shoes, and often had foot and leg fixations. Nurse Wolf's explanation was that long ago, when these big men were tiny and impressionable, this was the angle they caught, looking up at a real mommy.

I wondered whether babies – or any of these people – had orgasms. After all, wasn't that the point?

'No. I see a lot of people who are denied that. That's part of the treatment. They're sent out without any release. I think there's also a liberating feeling of completely relinquishing your power.'

She did not find it odd that most of the people she saw were very successful. 'It's a vacation for them to be controlled, to be told what to do – to give pleasure to someone else. I don't engage in any overtly sexual stuff at all, but I can train someone to give the best foot massage.'

One of her most powerful clients came in once a week to submit to Nurse Wolf. His particular fetish was to be a sissy slave and to make her happy. Time was of no importance – five minutes, an hour, five hours: his kink was serving. He was not tied up. He was not restrained, though he did wear a leather collar. He also wore panties. Pleasure for this captain of industry was nearly always crouching in his collar and pink panties and painting her toenails.

He happened to be a businessman. She saw many such men. She had noticed that the soberest and straightest-looking businessmen had a passion for secret tattoos and hidden piercings. She suspected that the ones from out of town arranged New York business meetings in order to see her. They would call and say, 'I've got a window between five and seven. I'm definitely coming.'

If they said, 'Do you have any special instructions for me beforehand?' Nurse Wolf would reply, 'Go to Victoria's Secret – get satin panties. Get this colour nail polish. Wear the panties. Get your toenails painted by the time you're here.' And they would obey.

***

Some of this was so harmless it was almost lovable. The babies, the pedicurist in his panties, the cross-dressers, the obedient attorneys. There was no pain, nothing of what Nurse Wolf would call 'heavy corporal', only role-play. The determinants were cultural as well as in our personal history. In Nurse Wolf's studio there was no censor, no political correctness. No ethnic group was spared and, predictably, the most victimised ethnic groups acted out their fantasies in what Nurse Wolf called 'the psycho-drama' of role-playing. This was related to the

Englishman's 'cutely developed sense of kink' and his reliving the exquisite humiliation of a public school caning; but it went further. In this sense her dungeon was an artefact of the mainstream, something influenced by the ethnicity in child-rearing – the nanny–mommy nexus, the spanking ethic. But darker fantasies were induced by racial history. It was not for Nurse Wolf to condemn; on the contrary, it was one of the paradoxes of her sadism that she was obliged to become a willing partner – many of the fantasies were imposed on her.

Whenever I mentioned the mothering, the dressing-up, the ritual punishments that were common in the most Apple Pie-eating American households, she talked about how inventive Jews and Catholics could be, because of the repressiveness in their upbringing. They were intensely fetishistic.

I had wondered whether she saw any African-Americans. Yes, she said, she did. Like the Nazi interrogation demanded by the Jewish clients, the role-playing and submission asked for by African-Americans were among the darker desires of her clients.

'I see two black men, both in their late sixties. They're into heavy bondage – abduction scenarios. The scene is in Botswana. They are sneaking around and peeking at me. I've got to capture them and tie them up. He's screaming, "Don't tie me up!"'

One of them she met at an S&M party some years ago. A friend of hers said, 'I want you to meet my slave.' The black man was tied up and being verbally abused ('You little nigger'), while having cigarette ash flicked at his head.

I said, 'Doesn't this go against everything you believe?'

'If you know where something's coming from, and you both enter into a situation where you can explore things that are really dark, it's more pure in a way. I had to ascertain really quickly: is this guy sound of mind? Is this going to destroy him? Is this going to do something destructive? When I make that determination it's by mutual agreement.'

'How was he dressed?'

The man was naked, facedown on a table and at four points tied down, spread-eagled. The other mistresses came over and beat him.

'I leaned over and whispered, "I saw you looking at her milky-white breasts. What were you thinking about?"'

They took turns beating him.

'We had a great experience,' Nurse Wolf said, 'but I crossed a real line for myself. I was saying, "You wanna go here? Then go here – and it might be a lot further than you anticipated." I couldn't say to this guy, "Have a positive feeling about yourself."'

When Nurse Wolf told me she was especially fond of

her Japanese clients, I told her about *Pink Samurai*, a detailed book about eroticism in Japanese life, the slave-girl fantasies which involve torture, the schoolgirl fantasies in which soiled panties figure – selling panties is a sideline for many entrepreneurial Japanese schoolgirls. As for the defecation fantasies, Nurse Wolf said that her Japanese clients had never expressed any interest, but that she had wanted to see what it was all about.

A woman came in and did sessions, a few of them. Nurse Wolf understood her own limits then. She was revolted by it. Telling me the story her face was fixed in a look of utter disgust.

'I have a couple of great Japanese clients. My Japanese are totally into being punished. I know this Japanese guy who is into serious rope bondage. Japanese rope bondage is really beautiful, and each rope has a purpose, it's creative, it's really satisfying. Sometimes, just to learn, I've switched roles – it's great. But I want to be doted on, I want to be dominant.'

***

Not all the clients visited alone. 'How do I get my wife interested in this?' was a common question that Nurse Wolf had to answer. She urged them to bring the woman in – wife or girlfriend. Nurse Wolf said that she dominated the men while the women watched, and often the women became excited – watching the man being forcibly cross-dressed, or expertly humiliated, or whipped. Nurse Wolf sometimes made the man serve the wife or lover; tied the man up – head bondage, whatever – and forced him to be the woman's sex slave. Some women became obsessed and ended up caning their men with startling gusto. A loved-one's connivance was an advantage, since most of her clients were forced to be covert. It posed a problem if a man wished his taste for pain to be hidden from his wife or girlfriend. Were they going to be able to take their clothes off for a month? Nurse Wolf asked rhetorically.

'One man had to go home with a perfect handprint on his face. He had to come up with a mugging story. Or rope burns on the wrist, or mask lines are another – someone sweating in a black leather mask and they have stains on their face. A whip is likely to wrap around the thigh and cause obvious bruising.'

Several couples requested a branding. This was more Blacksmith Betty than Nurse Wolf, though medicine played a part. She heated a piece of metal and let it cool a little and then branded the man on his buttocks, scarring him for life – but that was the intention. Another man was branded with his wife's name.

Cutting was 'blood play'. This called for a medical-room session and, as well as satisfying the man's masochism, it called upon all the resources of Nurse Wolf in her Wicked Nurse role.

'I do a fair amount of cutting and sewing,' Nurse Wolf said, describing the actual suturing. 'I might sew the penis to the leg, or do cuts around the nipples, or the arms.'

When I seemed alarmed by her mention of scalpels and suturing, she said she did not cut deep or do anything risky. But surely sewing a man's penis to his leg did not fall into the category of mother's sense of fun?

'It's only dangerous if you don't sew it with enough stitches, and they pull out. You sew all the skin. You have to attach it at enough points so that the likelihood of it pulling out is not great. There's only a few people that I do it with. And the idea is that they go out to dinner with their other mistress, or call-girl, or whatever, and they have to stay in that position. I've sutured nipples and wrapped the sutures around their neck so that if they didn't stay in a certain position it was painful, and it was difficult for them to, say, put their coat on. So it's a continual public humiliation.'

One novelty was her sewing a man's foreskin together at the end and then sewing a button to it. The man loved it. She was amazed by the pain levels he could endure. He went out to dinner afterwards with an Asian woman ('Not a hooker, I can tell'). The woman was part of the treatment. The whole point was that he was not allowed release. The woman brought snippers and after dinner she snipped off the sutures.

Hearing about this painful procedure I winced and said, 'Isn't this dangerous? Any of these things could hurt someone if used to excess. I mean, you can die.'

Nurse Wolf became visibly upset and covered her face. 'Please don't say that. Touch something! I don't want that negative stuff around here. I've had virtual 911 [999] experiences. Really scary. And I do a lot of really heavy things. I mean, if someone's hooked up to an electrical device and they're hanging on my suspension in the other room – if someone's hanging by their ankles and they pass out, that's a big responsibility. Or there are the ones I electrocute. I use a TENS unit – it's a thing for nerve stim-ulation – little, like, jolts of electricity. It's been adapted for kinky use.'

This was Nurse Wolf at her darkest, wickedest. She described using this electric nerve-stimulator with its accessories, one of which was a catheter. Such equipment is offered for sale in the S & M magazines, a Master High Frequency Unit with a selection of electrodes for $189, along with 'authentic' prison wrist-shackles and leg-irons, 'enema and colonic supplies'.

'An electrified catheter of course has got to be sanitary. Got to swab carefully! The catheters come in different thicknesses. I insert it and switch on the electricity.'

This was popular with some clients, but now and then a man asked for something he couldn't handle.

'One guy is into very heavy bondage. I call it "cause and effect bondage". If he moves one way it hurts – for example a pierced nipple will move on a pierced testicle. He is always affecting his own pain-level too. If he's squirming from being caned on the ass he's going to feel other stuff. He's also into sensory deprivation, so the combination of all these things that he can't physically handle means that he's going to lose it some time. If he's not breathing properly in this state he's not going to be able to say, "I think I'm going to pass out."'

'What does he say?'

'I have some safe words. If something isn't working I have them say, "This isn't working." But I don't want them to control the session, like "Code Red" or "Mercy", because that way they're in control.'

'But what if they did say that?'

'Then I would back off. Because if they did say that, there's problems. But I'm into heavy chains. I don't want to waste my time. "A light whipping, please." Forget it. I'm old and jaded. I think, "What's that? You can't take that?" I was in one session with a guy and I said, "Look at you! You said you'd do anything for me! And you can't take it!"

'Dale was there, sitting in. I said to her, "Beat me. Use that on me to show him what an incredible wuss he is –

such a baby." I changed places. I wanted to prove to him what a wuss he was. I was like, "I don't like this. I don't even do this, and I can take more than you!" '

A serious problem arose with one man who wanted to be wrestled into submission, facing two women wrestlers. Nurse Wolf, who was game for most activities, and had trained in boxing, teamed up with another woman in wrestling sessions.

Her name was 'Daisy'. She was on steroids. She was attractive and well-built and covered in tattoos. With a select and devoted clientele, she would fly around the country and do wrestling sessions. It was serious wrestling, in the hotel room, and it was private.

'We'd sometimes do tag-team. We'd go to, say, Ohio. I'd wear a long wig. We'd go to these Holiday Inn Courtyard hotels and do wrestling sessions. Sometimes we'd meet pilots or whoever in the bar and Daisy would say, "Hey want to wrestle for a couple of dead presidents? Got a couple of dead presidents on you?" She was great. The guys would be terrified.'

On one occasion at a Holiday Inn in Manhattan they met a teacher who had flown in from Canada for the session. It was almost a disaster.

'He was small – about 160. Daisy could bench-press him. She could hold him over her head. He was paying three or four hundred and I was getting a hundred. I was doing head scissors on this guy and I'm squeezing the fuck out of him. I'm squeezing his carotid artery and he passes out and gets a spasm.'

Meanwhile, Daisy was saying, 'He's fine, keep going!'

'His head is between my thighs and he's spasming. I was torturing him. I let him go and he dropped. I thought he was dead. He spasms and then he goes out and I'm thinking, "The guy's dead." Then Daisy slaps him really hard and does CPR on him. He comes back.'

The man was groggy and disoriented from having fainted, but when he realised where he was he said, 'Okay, let's go.' He wanted more.

'I couldn't believe it. I ended up putting my gloves on and beating the fuck out of him. "I hate you for almost dying!" I don't think he was happy with his black eye. His nose was bleeding. His lip was split. His nose was across his face. I loved it. Afterwards I made him take us out for sushi.'

There were other emergencies, many from friends who knew Nurse Wolf's cool head and resourcefulness in a crisis.

'I got this phone call from a guy I know and he says, "Something happened to me. I wrecked my ass." He was using some kind of dildo and ruptured something. He says, "I'm bleeding – what does it mean? There's a big lump. I think I've broken something."'

Nurse Wolf in her role as triage nurse said, 'Call GMHC,' – The Gay Men's Health Crisis – an inspired decision. The man called GMHC and was referred to a doctor who diagnosed his condition as serious and performed emergency surgery on him.

Another time she was with a man who was using a vibrator to sodomise himself. And the contraption, about four inches long, torpedo-shaped, simply disappeared. The man howled but she told him to be calm; she would remove it. But after trying everything – tweezers, forceps, even her barbecue tongs – the thing was somewhere inside him and the man was panicky. At this point Nurse Wolf had one of her flashes of insight.

'I sat him on the toilet and told him to push, and it came out, still buzzing.'

***

One day, we were in the restaurant of the Mark Hotel, having lunch, laughing over a menu item described as 'Weak Fish' – and Nurse Wolf was saying she certainly didn't want that. She was dressed in her working clothes – short leather skirt, pretty blouse, Doc Marten boots, a heavy chain around her neck, and there were young stylish women in the place who were dressed similarly, for this was the fashion – though probably those other women were not going to spend the rest of the afternoon dressing a banker as a sissy maid or breaking canes on an executive's buttocks, two sessions on Nurse Wolf's agenda. In this giggling about 'Weak Fish', Nurse Wolf used the expression 'real sex'.

'What did you say?' And I asked her to explain.

'Mutual reciprocity – real fucking. I love that too. I also like playing. I like slaves. I recommend both – real sex and role-play.'

It then occurred to me to ask whether these men ever begged to make love to her, just jolly jig-jig, cork-in-a-bottle-style sex. She was as shocked by this as she had been by the instance of kissing.

'They wouldn't dare. Are you kidding?' She made a fierce face me. 'They'd be dead. That's a line they'd never cross. Sure, there's some people who want to cross that line, but there's no way.'

'Still, your boyfriend knows about this. And it must be difficult to go from this – a man being bound up and humiliated – to see your boyfriend, have a drink, and so forth. Then go to bed? Is that transition difficult?'

'It depends on the day. Mostly it's the phone ringing off the hook – people being very needy. I had to take the cellphone to bed because I was expecting a call, and that was a big problem with my boyfriend. I have always done whatever I wanted to do. That's the first time I've ever had to be considerate of someone.'

Her boyfriend would get turned off after they had spent a nice day together and she had to go to the studio for a session. He'd say, 'You're going to work.' She said she knew he used that word because her word for it was 'play'.

Boyfriends came and went, but the other men had remained loyal through the years – she thought of them less as clients than as men she played with. As for sessions with women – in ten years she had seen only two women on their own, professionally. Her explanation was that women were less inclined to pay for this experience because they could get it in their own lives. It was much more difficult for men to get someone to play with them.

'Do you see yourself doing more of this, or less?'

'I can't do this for ever. I get more selective, more specific about what I want to do and what I don't want to do. There are people who call and I say, "I think you're a great person but I just can't do this session." This year I have been cleaning house.'

***

After so much pain it was, at last, not pain that truly upset Nurse Wolf but the spoken word. Perhaps I should have been warned when she spoke of her objection to foul name-calling or her exaggerated response to a dish called 'Weak Fish'. Words were much more powerful to her – and to some of her clients – than any whip. I happened to be

61

reading a new translation (by Husain Haddawy) of *The Arabian Nights* round about the time Nurse Wolf told me of her storytelling clients. These tales have been circulating since the ninth century and were written down about 600 years ago. They have as their point of departure the adulterous debauchery of King Shahrayer's wife with her lover, the black slave Mas'ud, and others. Ten black slaves dressed in women's clothes leap into the palace garden. 'Then the ten black slaves mounted the ten slave girls while the lady called "Mas'ud, Mas'ud!" and a black slave jumped from the tree to the ground, rushed to her, and raising her legs, went between her thighs and made love to her. Mas'ud topped the lady, while the ten slaves topped the ten girls, and they carried on till noon.'

King Shahrayer, after witnessing one of these orgies, kills his wife and decides that there is not a chaste woman on earth. As a further act of revenge he sleeps with a different woman every night and in the morning has her killed. Shahrazad, daughter of his Vizier, tries to save herself and the rest of womanhood by spending each night with the king and bewitching him with a new story. The stories in their untidied-up versions involve sex, sadism, kidnapping and mutilation. In the story of 'The Flogged One' a young wife is asked for a kiss by a handsome merchant. The woman turns her face to the merchant. 'He put his mouth on my cheek and bit off with his teeth a piece of my flesh.' The woman's outraged husband orders the woman to be punished. She is stripped, flogged and branded.

Nurse Wolf had her Shahrazads. It was role-play so strange that even she became upset; because she was not passive, she participated in the storytelling – she was sometimes Shahrazad. The most extreme examples of these sessions involved some of her longest-term clients, the ones she called 'the cannibals'.

One was a man with a Hansel & Gretel fantasy. With Nurse Wolf's assistance he fantasised about being a little boy and being cooked alive in a big pot. His fantasy was full of folk-tale ornamentation: the shadowy cottage, the dark woods, the witch's kitchen. At a certain point the man was eaten and the prospect of being chewed – his body being the main course – sexually aroused him, especially when Nurse Wolf helped with variations.

Another man, a very old man, also saw her to relate stories of cannibalism that would not be out of place in the later, weirder episodes of *The Arabian Nights*. His were similarly serial in nature, and like Shahrazad's, stories within stories. His basic fantasy revolved around the understanding that Nurse Wolf and he were in charge of a tropical island. Young women were abducted and taken to the island where they were fed and fattened and prepared for a Hawaiian feast, a luau. The fantasy included a French chef, a guest list, and lots of speculation.

This variation on Shahrazad fascinated me, especially the necessity for Nurse Wolf to suggest or elaborate a new plot twist each time the Island Cannibal showed up for a session. It was certainly literary and seemed to belong to an old tradition of storytelling: the tale intended literally to pass time and to captivate the listener. The way I saw it, the Cannibal – in indulging in these serial fantasies – was perhaps prevented from going out and killing and eating a woman; Nurse Wolf's assistance in his storytelling was a way of protecting womanhood from anthropophagy. Both Nurse Wolf and the Cannibal talked, but the burden was always upon Nurse Wolf to find new aspects of the story to explore. This Island Cannibal story has gone on for eight years. Were it printed it would fill many volumes.

'It wasn't scary for the first six or seven years,' Nurse Wolf said, 'but lately it's started scaring me. I don't think about it beforehand, but when he shows up I think: maybe we'll have a hunt for her this time, or the woman is roasting on the spit, or we'll have an auction and serve up portions that people have bought.'

'Is it a particular type of woman he's after?'

'He's very specific. There's a lot of detailed things. They have to be between 18 and 20. They have to have a good shape. He's got to measure you. One day he brought a tape measure and he measured my arm, "Like this."'

Sometimes the Cannibal brought books to the session, with titles like *Aladdin's Slave Farm*, about girls who are kidnapped by cannibals.

The preparation of the meal was more important to the Cannibal than the eating, but it was always understood that a woman was being kept for later.

'We trick them. They think they're going to be sex slaves. They are very carefully groomed, and they are kept in cells together. They are not allowed to speak to each other. They are graded. They are constantly evaluated. They are given daily punishments. They are completely broken down and made to be submissive, and then when they're prepared we go into a detailed plan about the arrival of the guests, about how many we're going to have, and what we're going to serve at the luau – the arrival, and roasting of the girls, and then they'll baste them, all our guests will baste the girl. We've had many discussions – I wonder how I can even go here sometimes? – about what is the consistency of their flesh if they die in fear? A logical question. I mean these people at the luau are spending a lot of money, right?'

Now and then, while role-playing, Nurse Wolf let the Cannibal bite her. 'He doesn't break the skin. He's got Parkinson's Disease and his teeth are shaking. He's got dentures! He bites my arm. He's standing – he bites my bicep, and he's like touching himself and it's a sick thrill for him. I am in charge. I am, like, "Bite me. It's tender here." He takes out his little tape measure. I say, "You can get the most meat off the upper arm. Or here... Or here..."'

'Is there anything in it for you?'

'I am bringing something I like to it. You've got to realise my "freak factor". The thrill for me is I am exhilarated by Parkinson's Disease and dentures – and he's out of this snowy-haired, poly-knit, Poligrip ad and instead of playing tennis with his wife he's biting me and having cannibal fantasies. I mean, this is someone's grandfather! Biting me! My arm! It's not about me and it's not about him. I think about it and I snicker. I try to block the ugliness of it.'

The man, who was in his late seventies, was so aroused by the sessions that he began calling her nearly every day and imploring Nurse Wolf to see him three times a week. She couldn't face it.

'I am up for seeing him every two or three weeks. He totally drains me. It's the reality of it. That I am helping him in his fantasy. But it's so dark. I don't get anything back from him. I get sucked dry. A lot of people feed my imagination. But after a session he changes like Jekyll and Hyde and I just leave the room. It's so embarrassing. I was never into the words. I visualised things and I thought: "What a great story." But I realised that I

66

could never eat after it. That I dreaded it sometimes.'

Yet the man, the Cannibal, was helped. It was possible to see this Shahrazad role-playing as the apotheosis of the dominatrix as nurse. There was first the fact that by verbalising his cannibal fantasies he was sublimating them and not acting on them. Horrific as the words sounded, their very utterance perhaps prevented the man from eating women.

And there was the interesting fact of Parkinson's. Oliver Sacks, who has studied Parkinsonian patients, has said that a person who is suffering the mental or physical rigidity associated with the disease often finds release in closely observing another person. The symptoms of Parkinson's are alleviated by 'borrowing' language and gestures from someone else. Nurse Wolf provided that for the Parkinsonian Cannibal; she loaned him her language and gesture. Though she has no idea that the studies supporting this process are still being researched, she was helping the Parkinsonian Cannibal to function.

Nurse Wolf was not sure about this when I mentioned it, and anyway the whole subject of cannibalism upset her.

'I always think, "One step beyond biting is eating."'

'Why do you let him bite you?'

Nurse Wolf said, 'I think it's the Mommy in me!' And she laughed, but after that outburst she grew gloomy and said, 'I am constantly told that I don't see a good representative cross-section of men. "You are not in the normal world where you can make judgments on things – or make generalisations."'

But it seemed to me that the opposite was true. She understood what most men were really like. True, the covert and the rejected sought her out – no one else would see them. You immediately think of a long queue of jostling grotesques and twisted old fruits from George Grosz or Francis Bacon. But no, lined up, they were people who were instantly familiar – the electrician, the insurance executive, the construction worker, the stock-broker, the editor, the writer, the white-haired grandpa. The hooded man was hooded precisely because anyone might recognise him.

We did not know much about them, but Nurse Wolf knew everything. Enigmatic to their wives and girlfriends, hearty and humorous to children and grandchildren, it was exclusively to her that they divulged their secrets.

'One of my slaves was terminally ill,' she said to me one day. 'He told me – almost a year before he told his family. So he and I had this secret; I was the only person who knew.'

She went on beating him. He was one of the men who liked 'heavy corporal'. He kept seeing Nurse Wolf, to be beaten, right up to the month before he died.

This moved me. She told me how much it meant to

her to know his secret. She grew fond of seeing him; she looked forward to whipping him. She wept when he died.

It was one of the strangest stories I had ever heard; it was as much about strength as it was about human frailty. It was also about that middle ground of connivance where there is hardly a difference between nurse and patient.

I said, 'So it's almost like having a relationship.'

'Not "like". It is a relationship,' she said.

Photograph: Elena Seibert

DR SACKS

Oliver Sacks was sipping tea, juggling a cookie, his knees together, his fumbling hands making him seem unsure and a bit hunted, like Edward Lear – the same Socratic beard, the same gaze, twinkling with myopia – and stammering his gratitude to the host, who was a stranger to him. Oliver looked lost, like a big befuddled and bearded boy.

Famously absent-minded, the next minute Oliver was preoccupied with some papers he thought he had mislaid. He slapped his pockets. 'Bugger,' he muttered. I was thinking: where has his cookie gone to? Oliver said, 'And where are my car keys? What have I done with my keys?' The hostess was active, talking most of the time about something else, with wearying intensity, while Oliver fussed, rummaging for his lost papers, his lost keys. 'No, that's not it – that's my biscuit,' Oliver said, pulling cookie crumbs from his pocket. He was the picture of confusion. His shirt had become untucked because of his muscular shoulders, and yet he looked schoolboyish, desperate, as he foundered. Even his dimples had been sucked flat in an expression of pure panic. Then, sighing with relief, he put his hands on the papers, and the keys too.

A few minutes later we were in the street.

'What did you make of her?' I asked, referring to the hostess.

A calm descended on Oliver. He had tucked in his shirt. He weighed his car keys in his hand. He said in a diagnostic tone, 'Frail, yet explosive. Definitely compulsive. Possibly – though this might be a bit strong, this word might need refining – psychotic. I wouldn't like to be around her when she goes off. But I'd like to see her again.'

In the crispest way he had precisely summed up the woman we had casually met. Even slapping cookie crumbs in his pockets and fearing the worst for his keys, he is the most perceptive of men. There is something of Sherlock Holmes in his shrewd summing-up of scattered neurological clues, and it is probably appropriate, since Arthur Conan Doyle based Holmes's deductive ability on one of his medical schoolteachers, a hawk-eyed diagnostician. Oliver has that concentration, and his 'street neurology' was something I had longed to see ever since I read about it in 'The Possessed' chapter of *The Man Who Mistook His Wife for a Hat*. The phrase 'street neurology' refers to the assessment of a person's condition after observing their behaviour in a casual setting – the street, a bus, a movie-line, a room full of strangers.

Among the many antecedents of 'street neurology', Oliver said, was James Parkinson who 'delineated the disease that bears his name, not in his office, but in the teeming streets of London'. And for the illness to be understood it had to be seen in the world. This was perhaps truer of Tourette's Syndrome. The preface to the seminal book *Tics* (1901) by Meige and Feindel described a ticqueur in the streets of Paris. 'The clinic, the laboratory, the ward are all designed to restrain and focus behaviour.' A clinic could be scientific and helpful, but Oliver advocated a more open 'naturalistic neurology'.

One day after seeing 'Witty Ticcy Ray', Oliver's first Touretter, Oliver saw three Touretters on the streets of New York. A woman of about 60, the most 'florid' of the three, seemed to be convulsing or having a fit; in fact, her mode of Tourette's was the compulsive caricaturing in an accelerated and parodic way of everyone who passed by her. She was possessed by each person for an instant: 'In the course of a short city-block this frantic old woman frenetically caricatured the features of 40 or 50 passers-by.' The whole sequence of possessions took little more than two minutes.

Seen in the street, the particularities of the woman's condition were more obvious than they would have been in a clinic. For variety and context, Oliver said, there was really no better place for observing people 'than a street in New York – an anonymous public street in a vast city – where the subject of extravagant, impulsive disorders can enjoy and exhibit to the full the monstrous liberty, or slavery, of their condition'.

I asked Oliver about this the first time I met him, about four years ago. He said to me, 'I had a Tourette's patient in my office. I talked with him and saw quite a lot of him. But I thought, "What is this man's life like?" So we went outside. I saw him in the street, in the world. Then I understood him much better.'

**

A writer's life is almost unapproachable except through the writing, which is inevitably full of ambiguities. You spend time with a writer and you get – what? – wool-gathering, silences, rants, evasions, the contents of a cracker barrel; anyway, most such visits are just excursions into tendentiousness. But if the writer also happens to be a doctor there is a visible and unambiguous human dimension that can be seized: Voltaire squeezing leeches on to a patient's skin, Chekhov poking someone's tonsils, Freud closely questioning the hysterical Anna M., William Carlos Williams delivering a baby. Oliver Sacks happens to be a marvellous writer, with a range of expression that is both exact and poetic, his neurological writings have been praised by no less a stylist than W. H. Auden. Even Oliver's footnotes fascinate; the footnotes to his *Island of the Color-Blind* are wonderfully informative and original, with a casual brilliance. For a footnote in his essay on the scientist Sir Humphry Davy, his point of departure is the little-known fact that the poet Coleridge attended Davy's lectures; he speaks in the footnote of how other poets have been lovers of scientific language:

> Coleridge was not the only poet to renew his stock of metaphors with images from chemistry. The chemical phrase 'elective affinities' was given an erotic connotation by Goethe; 'energy' became for Blake, 'eternal delight'; Keats, trained in medicine, revelled in chemical metaphors. Eliot, in 'Tradition and the Individual Talent', employs chemical metaphors from beginning to end, culminating in a grand 'Davyan' metaphor for the poet's mind: 'The analogy is that of the catalyst...The mind of the poet is the shred of platinum.' One wonders whether Eliot knew that his central metaphor, catalysis, was discovered by Humphry Davy in 1816. A wonderful metaphoric use of chemistry is Primo Levi's *The Periodic Table*. Levi was himself both a chemist and a writer.

I mentioned to Oliver that the composer Borodin had been trained as a chemist. But of course he knew that.

'Borodin was a friend of Mendeleev,' he said. The literary references in his piece about a chemist are not gratuitous. The pathology of literature is one of Oliver's favourite subjects, and he has published a paper in the *British Journal of Medicine* about 'Tourette's and Creativity'. He has brought his neurological experience to bear on such figures as Dostoyevsky, Bartok, Kierkegaard, Mozart, Nabokov, Klee, DiChirico. 'Samuel Johnson was probably Tourettic,' he has said, 'Sherlock Holmes possibly autistic.' The visionary mystic Hildegarde of Bingen Oliver diagnoses as 'migrainous' in his book *Migraine*. One of her visions, 'The Fall of the Angels', is a shower of stars, which she describes with lyrical rapture. Doctor Sacks notes that Hildegarde has experienced a severe migraine and 'a shower of phosphenes in transit across her visual field, their passage being succeeded by a negative scotoma'. He is profoundly sympathetic and even admiring of the episode, and he adds in brilliant interpretation, 'Invested with this sense of ecstasy, burning with profound theophorous and philosophical significance, Hildegarde's visions were instrumental in directing her towards a life of holiness and mysticism. They provide a unique example of the manner in which a physiological event, banal, hateful or meaningless to the vast majority of people, can become in a privileged consciousness, the substrate of a supreme ecstatic inspiration.'

One of the many satisfactions in spending time with Oliver Sacks is hearing such an astonishing range of references, each one a little glimpse into his erudition and his life. 'Something that repels me about damascene blades is that after heating the steel they used to quench it by shoving them into the bodies of slaves.' Or, 'Mendeleev had a dream in which he saw the arrangement of the Periodic Table. In the morning he wrote it down... I had an intense boyhood interest in metals... I dreamed of manganese one night...They use beryllium for the nose cones of rockets.' Or 'Nabokov has a lovely description about trees in winter looking like the nervous systems of giants.'

I also liked the references which were flashes of other Olivers: Oliver, the word-lover ('festination', 'volant', 'apodictic'); Oliver, the confidante of Thom Gunn, A.R. Luria, W.H. Auden; Oliver, the weightlifter (he held a California weightlifting record – doing a full squat with 600 pounds); Oliver, the motorcyclist with an extensive knowledge of classic English machines like the Norton he used to own, as well as esoteric motorcycle writings (T.E. Lawrence's *The Mint*, for example); Oliver, as Wolf Sacks – using his middle name for its lycanthropic associations, consultant physician to a California chapter of the Hell's Angels; Oliver, the former dabbler in hallucinogenic drugs and morning glories.

His 'druggy excitements' ended on the last day of

1965, when he looked into a mirror, saw his skeletal self and said, '"Unless you stop you will not see another New Year." And I stopped.'

One day we were talking about autism. Oliver said, 'When I was at a summer camp in Canada for autistic and Tourettic children one of them saw a goat and asked, "Is it a diagram?" Imagine the degree of alienation! I wonder whether with the largest dose of LSD possible one would ever see a goat as a diagram?'

'Probably, very easily,' I said. 'But I don't know. I have never taken LSD.'

'Oh, I have. It wouldn't produce that hallucination,' he said. 'One time at my house in Topanga Canyon after a huge overdose of Morning Glories I thought the cacti were gigantic insects – gigantic motionless insects. Still an insect is a living thing, whereas a diagram is an abstraction.'

Or this sort of conversation, animadverting about the brain: 'Those so-called Aztec Bird-Men that were exhibited in circuses? They were microcephalic. The face was normal size but the head went back like this' – he squinched his face small in imitation of the weirdly tiny heads. 'They were exhibited with Macrocephalics.'

These strange skulls were also exhibited in the Royal College of Surgeons Museum, where Oliver's mother used to take him, to show him other oddities, such as The Irish

Giant and the 20-inch Sicilian woman who weighed 17 pounds. Oliver can still recall their names – Patrick Cotter and Caroline Crachami.

'Does a microcephalic person have language?' I had asked.

'Oh, yes, the brain may be smaller than a cat's but they have language. Brain sizes are interesting. Turgenev's endocranial cast is 2100cc, versus Anatole France who had barely 1000 ccs of brain.'

'So brain size doesn't matter?'

'I am not saying that. I am saying that in the severest human idiocy there is always some language. Especially language. The microcephalic person may be a lot less intelligent than the average chimp, yet they are human, they will have some language.'

Chimp language is another of his scientific interests. In *Seeing Voices*, Oliver discusses the question of whether chimps have language. 'It seems they don't,' and though they can make certain guttural signifying sounds, their method of communication is a 'gestural code'.

There seemed nothing he did not know, or had not seen, or experienced.

***

But Oliver, the doctor, was the person I wanted to know better: Oliver in a ward, Oliver making a house-call,

Oliver on the street, on the move, in the world, observing; especially Oliver in New York, treating patients. It is obvious from his writing – and he has himself said explicitly – that 'patients' is a misleading word for the people he writes about: they are his friends, some as dear to him as family members, and that he has gained understanding by having developed his relationships with these people over many years.

Oliver's bumbling is not an act, nor a deliberate diversion. He really is near-sighted and cack-handed. He constantly loses things. He is hesitant and forgetful; in his dreamiest and perhaps most intellectually productive moods he stumbles and trips. He has fallen on his face and sustained many serious injuries. He wrote a whole book, *A Leg to Stand On*, about one bad stumble, which resulted in a severe leg injury. Looking at the waves on a Hawaiian beach he shook his head and said to me, 'I can't swim there. If I got into those waves I'd end up a quadriplegic.'

Once in the water he never falters. Distance swimming, snorkelling, diving, he is a porpoise. I have swum with him in the dankest waters of Lewis Bay in Hyannis and Waimea Bay in Hawaii. He is a strong swimmer and stays in the water for a long time. 'It takes 40 minutes in the water just to warm up, and then the real swimming starts.'

He says he is happier among invertebrates, among cephalopods; among plants – ferns and cycads. One of his dreams is to swim in the so-called Jellyfish Lake on one of the Rock Islands of Palau, in the Western Pacific. I described to Oliver how I had swum there myself; the water was thick and yellowish, a stew of jellyfish, some like parasols and some like night-caps. They had no sting but they bulged with gelatinous ectoplasm and filled the small volcanic pool. My whole body was pressed at each stroke by the strongest wobble of slime, my fingers tangling in their greenish masses of tentacles. I did it on a dare and was glad finally to pull myself out of the water. Oliver said there was nothing he relished more than the thought of spending a whole day swimming among the millions of jellyfish.

On dry land he is less certain. He is a careful, if over-cautious driver. His bumper sticker reads 'American Fern Society'. The decal in his window says, 'British Pteridological Society'. Fluctuating temperatures make him irritable. He complains if the temperature inside or out does not hover around 65 degrees, and has been known to carry a foot-long thermometer into restaurants, especially in the summer, to establish at the outset whether the dining experience will be a comfortable one. He cannot cook. But he is not fussy about food, indeed he dislikes culinary variety. One of his unshakable habits is to eat the same meal every day. A large pot of the stuff is prepared for him at the weekend, and he warms up portions of it through the week. He is not odd in this, and, as Oliver would be the first to point out, most of the world's people eat the same meals every day. When I visited him at his bungalow on City Island in the Bronx, about an hour north of mid-town Manhattan, I saw a selection of ferns on the kitchen table, and stacks of books on his stove-top: the thick exhaustive *Dictionary of Applied Chemistry* and some others on the front burner, and a tome simply titled *Manganese* on the back burner.

Until he moved to the West Village, he spent part of the week at that house (which he bought in 1980 for its nearness to swimming and his hospitals). Apart from books, Oliver says, 'I own nothing of value.' His New York apartment is Sacks Central, both a comfortable apartment and an efficient office. Oliver types swiftly – as fast as his secretary – with two fingers on an old manual typewriter, but in his office he has access to every modern innovation, not just machines and computers and databases and a secretary, but Kate Edgar – assistant, minder, amanuensis and friend; and midwife to his last five books. Like many people with active minds, he is a bad enough sleeper to rank as an insomniac. He is tall, powerfully built from his daily swimming; he is physically strong, but he also carries on his body the bumps and scars and stitch-marks of his mishaps.

Oliver is at ease working in the hospital but says he

is sometimes wary, even there. He says that he fears that he might become very flustered one day at a hospital and, because of his stammering and shyness, he will be confused with a patient and get locked up.

'Without my badge and my white coat I am indistinguishable from many patients here,' he said to me. 'In Bronx State, a state mental hospital I used to work at, I always used to carry my white coat and my identity pass, because I was never sure that if I lost it I would be able to prove my sanity.'

'Oh, yes, yes,' he says mimicking a sarcastic doctor, 'Delusion of being Oliver Sacks.'

It is the nightmare of Chekhov's 'Ward Number 6', a story Oliver often refers to – in which the doctor, Andrei Yefimich Ragin, mistaken for a mental patient, is unable to talk his way out of the ward and he is left there, and beaten by a brutal watchman, while the other doctors smile at the poor doctor's protestations. One of the characteristics of a strong protest is that it sounds delusional and paranoid. 'I must go out!' he cries. He is told to shut up. He is beaten repeatedly and at last the doctor dies in his own hospital.

A cruel variation on this is the story Oliver tells about the former medical director of Beth Abraham Hospital in the Bronx, who had retired. Three years later this doctor was admitted to the same hospital with symptoms of an advancing dementia. One day returning to his old habits, this man slipped into his white coat and went to his old office and began scrutinising the patients' charts. Over one complex chart he muttered, 'Poor bugger', then closed it up and when he did he saw his own name on the file. He exclaimed, 'My God!' and turned completely ashen. He started shaking and crying in horror, seeing that he was the patient – with an irreversible dementia – and not the director. In that terrible lucid moment he saw it all.

'It was one of the most awful things I have ever seen. One out of a nightmare. He was devastated. Ultimately he became profoundly demented,' Oliver said, finishing his story with a grim sense that one of the paradoxes of neurology is that there is not always a clear distinction between sanity and madness – one often resembles the other, transformation is constant. Many people in the hospital could function on the street, many people on the street are demented.

***

Oliver's parents, Samuel and Elise Sacks were physicians and, just as important, they were 'medical storytellers' – seeing their patients as long-standing friends, with complex histories. Elise's father had 18 children and there were nearly a hundred first cousins. On his father's side, the Israeli elder statesman Abba Eban is Oliver's cousin, so was the cartoonist Al Capp. Oliver, the youngest of four boys, was a lonely member of this vast extended family. At the onset of the Blitz, in 1939, he was sent out of London for safety's sake. He was just six. It was to be a four-year ordeal of separation. He was exiled and isolated; he experienced physical cruelty, discomfort, the wintry mendacity of authority figures. He was first in a boarding house in Bournemouth and then – a further disruption – was moved to Brayfield, near Northampton.

This painful period in Oliver's life could have destroyed him. It certainly marked him, as the Blacking Factory marked Dickens, and the House of Desolation (fictionalised in 'Baa, Baa, Black Sheep') marked Kipling. It also sharply resembles the rustication that Orwell recounted in 'Such, Such, Were the Joys'. It was a form of child abuse verging on soul murder, in the phrase of Dr Leonard Shengold (a close friend of Oliver's) who discusses such traumas in his book *Soul Murder*.

'I became obsessed with numbers, as the only things I could trust,' Oliver says. He was reassured by the Periodic Table, seeing 'order and harmony in the family of elements'.

By wounding him, the experience made him the sort of scientist who is brother to the poet. In his childhood attachment to the Periodic Table, to colours, to metals, to science and solitude, he related to Humphry Davy, a kindred soul. As a university undergraduate in the late 1950s Oliver experienced England's first post-war sparkle, which was an intellectual rekindling that included the Angry Young Men, the Goons, and *Beyond the Fringe*. Jonathan Miller, who is almost an embodiment of that period's humour and intelligence and glamour, is one of Oliver's closest friends, and of course a fellow doctor.

Oliver moved to California just as America was being energised. He was 27 in San Francisco in the early 1960s, where everything was happening. He lived for five years in California – years of medical residence and reading; years of experiment; motorcycle years. Nineteen sixty-five was devoted to the study of earthworms at the Albert Einstein College of Medicine: he gathered worms by the thousand to extract myelia from their nerve cords, an episode that was inflated in the movie *Awakenings*.

In October 1966 he arrived at Beth Abraham Hospital, and there he has remained, working for 32 years, earning the New York rate of $12 for each patient he sees (though his income from books and lectures is substantial). This hospital, the 'Mount Carmel' of *Awakenings*, is in that hinterland of the Bronx, an hour or so from mid-town Manhattan by subway. Its nearest stop is Allerton Avenue. It was once a charity hospital. The patients here and at the hospital of the Little Sisters of the Poor not far away, where Oliver has been working since 1972, are generally older men and women.

Over the decades that Oliver has spent caring for these people, he has seen them age, sometimes showing improvements, sometimes degenerating or regressing. Many are in a kind of suspension. One brain-damaged man said to Oliver, 'I've recovered enough to know that I'll never recover enough.' Another man is immobilised in a chair. He was mugged in Manhattan in 1986, when he was 22, and received severe head injuries that put him in a coma. Afterwards treated in acute hospitals he improved a little. Now he is just sitting, a wounded man, but conscious of his condition.

I asked, 'Does he know where he is?'

Oliver said, 'He is aware enough to be enraged.'

'Agnes is our senior centenarian,' Oliver says, smiling at a bright-eyed woman in a wheelchair. 'Twenty years ago she chased me up four flights of stairs, vociferating. She was Parkinsonian. Violently, writhingly choreac' – Oliver has a habit, when using an expression such as 'writhingly choreac' of giving a deadly accurate imitation of the affliction – 'And, um, yes, I was frightened.'

One of the days I was at Beth Abraham, Oliver showed me a patient's thick record. This was Grace, also Parkinsonian; written in her file: 'An enigma since 1929'. Hers was a static neurological condition: writhing movements, tics, oscillation of the eyes. She was on no medication because one of Oliver's reiterated dictums is 'Ask not what disease the person has, but rather what person the disease has.'

Oliver observed that Grace felt an energy with her condition. 'With medication she would have devitalised.'

Her husband had been very important to her. Grace had said, 'I have the drive, he has the patience. We make a good pair.'

A note Oliver had made in Grace's record said, 'I cannot avoid the feeling that she is preparing for her death.' Grace died two months later.

Without the dullness induced by medication, a Parkinsonian patient has the possibility of the freedom to live; the energy to react, to 'borrow' postures or gestures from other people. ('Repetition can be an absorption of posture,' Oliver says.) Sometimes people are rigid until they see a friend, or an animal, or a pattern; until they hear music or are asked to go out for bagels.

Such patients, seemingly comatose or indifferent, react when they see Oliver. They smile, they widen their eyes. In many cases the first reaction of a patient is to reach out and touch him – he returns the touch, which is almost a caress. Many are rigid until they see Oliver and they become animated as he speaks to them, or hums a tune, or touches them. He embraces them, they hug him in return.

'Here is our Senior Resident,' says Oliver. 'Hello,

Horace' – and he clutches the man, who smiles shyly and says, 'Doctor Sacks.' Oliver holds his hand and speaks to him directly, softly, enquiring how he is.

Horace smiles. His arms and legs are stick-like, his fingers are twisted. He has a wan smile of innocence and sadness.

Horace has never walked. He has had cerebral palsy since birth. He was admitted in 1948, when he was 23 and the full name of the hospital was the Beth Abraham Home for Incurables. At the time he was selling newspapers in Times Square. He functioned fairly well and was a familiar sight on the corner of 42nd Street. American cities then were full of such newspaper vendors. He could sell papers, he could move his arms, he could speak and give change. Like many patients he had been looked after on the outside, but when he ceased to get help he was sent to Beth Abraham. He has been there now for 50 years, staring out the window. I remarked on the sadness in Horace's expression.

'He is rather sad now,' Oliver said. 'Horace was very attached to another patient, Ruth.' They sat side by side in their wheelchairs, holding hands. They ate together. 'Since Ruth died he has deteriorated. He has lost his goals.'

Outside the hospital, Oliver can become tongue-tied attempting to buy a ballpoint pen in a corner store, or appear helpless fiddling at the cash register in a coffee shop, his thick fingers futile and unresponsive in his coin purse. But he is alert and focused when he is seeing a patient – like the Tourettic surgeon and pilot he wrote about who never has tics when he is operating or flying a plane. In the hospital he is efficient, as completely at home as the patients, unshockable in a place that occasionally requires real nerve.

One day at Beth Abraham, Oliver and I were getting into the elevator with one of his colleagues when a woman wheeled herself at the opening, propelling herself towards the door, her left leg sticking straight out like the sort of weapon police reports ominously describe as 'a shod foot'. Her hair was tangled, she was old and energetic and angry.

'You fucking bastards!' she screamed at us. 'You bastards! Let me on the elevator! I want to get on! Let me fucking on! Fuck you!'

The door shut on the woman's howling. Everyone in the elevator was rattled, except Oliver, who said, softly with serene puzzlement, 'I think I recognise her. I am sure I know her. Didn't she used to be on the second floor? Ruth-something?'

A person's anger does not make Oliver angry; it appears to calm him and of course to make him more watchful, for rage is a symptom, like a tic or a gesture.

At the Little Sisters of the Poor Hospital, I was with

him when he saw Janet, a paranoid woman, who had been violent. Before Janet entered, the nurse gave Oliver the woman's records.

'She thinks there are men attacking her,' the nurse said. 'Men trying to rape her. She reported the priest and a workman – and I can tell you there was absolutely nothing in it. She's yelling and screaming.'

'Was the attacker on her right or her left?' Oliver said.

The nurse was not sure. I asked Oliver why he wondered this.

'She has a blind side, apparently,' he said, turning pages. 'Do you know the term "blind sight"? The sight that reaches consciousness. There are blind rats which don't fall off the edge of a table.'

Janet was about 70, with bulging thyroidal eyes and yellowy white hair in a small girl's page-boy cut, neatly dressed in slacks. Her puffy almost-coquettish face looked like Bette Davis's playing Baby Jane. She was eager to see Oliver, she had been waiting several days for his visit.

'Janet, isn't it? How are you doing, Janet?' Oliver said.

'There are a couple of men here who are bothering me,' Janet said, smiling at me. 'One of them is frightening me to death. Following me!'

'Yes?' Oliver said. 'On the left side or the right side?'

'On all sides! He ran out and tried to get me. He was being a smart aleck.'

Oliver said, 'What did he say?'

But the woman began to protest. 'I am a decent woman. I was raised in Greenwich Village by a good Irish family.' She said loudly, 'It wasn't as though I was wearing a bikini!'

'You said there were two men,' Oliver said.

'There's a Catholic brother – his shirt sticks out like it's a penis,' Janet said. 'He's staring and looking at me. This is a Catholic holy place! I dress modestly. I got into my room about ten at night. I was sleeping alone – I have to mention that. I have never married. All of a sudden I hear a fist banging on my room! I was afraid. After a while I looked out. No one there, but I saw Julia across the hall. Julia said, "It was the brother." The loud sound of fists on my door!' She said this looking at Oliver and me with popping eyes, smiling, smoothing the thighs of her slacks. She made Oliver promise to return soon, winked at me, and she left.

'Notice the erotic content in what she said,' Oliver said. '"I sleep alone." The mention of the bikini. The priest's shirt like a penis.'

Waiting for the woman's file afterwards, the nurse said, 'I forgot to tell you that when she is in her room she goes about stark naked. She answers the door without a stitch on. Just stands there in the doorway, naked.'

'Paranoia and eroticism often go together,' Oliver said,

making a note in the file. Each file is a detailed narration of a person's condition – a story; in many cases a long, episodic story.

He sees to the heart of the person. The first thing I learned at the hospital is that his patients are his friends. These are close relationships, developed over years. There is intense understanding and compassion. Perhaps no treatment is ever possible unless a human relationship is given a chance to develop.

'This woman can't speak, but she can sing,' Oliver said, as a smiling woman propelled her wheelchair towards him. He introduced me to the woman, Jane, and to the music therapist, Connie Tomaino.

Jane smiled and, as patients seem to do, clutched his hand, hugged his arm, but she said nothing. Oliver, who cannot sing, compensates for this by becoming a conductor. This does not always work. I could not accommodate him when, introducing me to a song-responsive patient, he said, 'Sing something by the Grateful Dead.'

Connie began to sing, 'What a friend we have in Jesus.'

Jane found her voice and joined the hymn, and the singing of it – regarding Oliver as she sang – was like a greeting. She became livelier, her facial expressions became friendly; she was for the duration of the hymn totally animated. When it ended she entered a sort of blankness. Jane was aphasic. She could utter one word – 'fine' – in conversation, but the rest was what a neurologist would describe as memory deficits. She could sing fluently.

Connie has found in her work over the past 20 years that memories aren't, it seems, really lost, at least with apparent aphasia or dementia. What is lost or damaged is the ability to access these memories.

'What music can do, or at least music that is familiar, is tap into those memories or unleash them. Sometimes the music is enough to cue those lost memories and bring them back to immediacy.'

Oliver read his notes from Jane's file: 'She is vehemently expressive despite her aphasia. She continues to be able to sing, to recite, she is an excellent musician and has an uproarious sense of humour. With the Lord's Prayer – the cadences continued, and the inner meaning, while the words degenerated into cadenced garble...'

I looked over his shoulder. In the record of a patient called Pearl, another doctor had written 'this demented woman' – and beside it Oliver had written almost scoldingly 'Not demented!'

Oliver stood aside and let his protégé speak. What looks like modesty or deference is a technique for creating a moment. Oliver's standing aside was part of his method for obliquely watching a patient react to strangers. Oliver encouraged me to talk – to interact: he seemed to like the thought that the patient and I were strangers; he let the patient speak. Oliver, the author of the paper 'Music and the Brain' (music helped him walk again when his leg was injured), said nothing, just smiled, watched all this, and then urged Connie to say something.

'First there is an initial recognition,' Connie said. The effect of music on a person with aphasia is strange at first for the patient. 'There is a possibility of connection, and an uncanny feeling of restlessness and uneasiness,' she said. 'It is like their being in a strange place. After that there are connections.'

One woman who was not verbal at all, who could not utter her own name, began talking about her son after hearing a certain piece of music.

After eight weeks of treatment, which was music therapy, she became verbal. The music that unlocked her memory was 'Does your mother come from Ireland?' Other Irish songs contributed to her fluency. She was in her mid-eighties, born in Ireland.

'I played recordings of songs that would have been popular in the 1930s,' Connie said. 'The first few sessions were only facial reactions – smiles and crying. I played "It's a long way to Tipperary" and she burst into tears.'

As Irish songs worked with this woman, Chinese songs worked with a Chinese man; and Latin songs with a Puerto Rican. Patients who were described as demented or aphasic remembered events and people and acquired a sort of comprehension of their personal history.

Oliver gestured towards an old woman slumped in a wheelchair. 'She may speak to you. Her voice is a little slurred and ataxic.'

'How long have you known her?'

'I have been seeing her since '66.'

Thirty-two years: one of the thousands of patients Oliver has seen and described minutely in hospital records; but who have not become subjects for his neuro-histories.

Oliver looked wistful. 'It's sort of sad in a way that we've never been able to make a radical change in her condition.'

Stefan, whom Oliver has known for 26 years, came in 1972. Stefan in a warm-up suit, sat aggressively in a wheelchair, leaning on his forearms, his face forward.

'I always think of Stefan as a young man with a lot of hair. And how does he see me?'

Stefan shook his head negatively when Oliver approached him.

Oliver said, 'I don't think he has ever forgiven me for bringing him here. But I wonder. Is his so-called schizophrenia itself an expression of his disease?'

Mild dementia, a stroke and a fall had incapacitated Gladys, a 70-year-old black woman. But it had been discovered that Gladys had played the piano in clubs in her time. A piano was found. Gladys recaptured an entire repertoire of songs, and while we stood there she played 'Moon River' and then 'The Birth of the Blues' and 'All the Things You Are' and 'Take the A Train', moving her fingers skilfully, playing from memory.

The other patients stopped gabbling. They sat up. They turned away from the television set. They listened, and when it was over they applauded.

'While the music was playing it wasn't a hospital,' Oliver said.

As Gladys had so vastly improved, I wondered whether the same happened to other patients.

'Sometimes,' Oliver said. 'I saw a chap this morning who is going to leave the hospital. I don't know whether he has improved so vastly. He was involved in a motor-vehicle accident. He was brain-injured but his wife has got a large settlement, so they will be able to manage. But it was for this reason that the post-encephalitics used to be so envied. People used to come up and say, "I wish I were post-encephalitic" – instead of having multiple-sclerosis or cerebral palsy or something – "because you could do something for me. I'd have a chance."'

I said, 'Does music treatment have any effect on Parkinson's patients?'

'Yes,' Connie said. 'In the case of Parkinson's it works

as "rhythmic cueing" – people get out of their chair and just start dancing.'

'What is the mechanism?'

Oliver said, 'People have trouble generating their own rhythm. Their sense of time is off. People with Parkinson's' sense of timing is off – you have to give them timing. Tempo. And it's an almost incorruptible tempo. Music imposes a tempo and prevents acceleration.'

'Or people can internalise a musical phrase and thereby know when they need to breathe. I did this with a small grant with people who had disarthria and other kinds of muscular damage. When they started they could only do three syllables. "How-are-you?" was the best they could do. By the time we finished, and this was only two months later, they were up to 19 syllables.'

'Did they also take medication?'

'No. It was learning a technique and listening, feeling it, breathing. But there was such an improvement people were asking "Did they have new medication?"'

Oliver said, 'People with Alzheimer's are able to play music very well. Why is one ability preserved and another lost? There are people who are too drunk to stand that dance well, and when the music stops they fall down.'

We left the ward. Oliver was smiling – he had loved the way the atmosphere of the ward had been trans-formed by the music. Three years before, introducing me to a hospital, Oliver had said to me, 'However sad or frightening, there is something positive here.'

**

Pursuing the idea of 'street neurology', I suggested walking around New York City, just looking at the people on the sidewalks – limping, twitching, 'vocalising'. To an outsider, New York City seems populated by people on the verge of a nervous breakdown; and a New York nutter seems to me world-class. Was this something to do with the way the city, so cellular, so like an asylum, an island of vertical compartments, isolates people and intensifies psychosis?

Dr Sacks might have the answer. In general, New Yorkers seem to me like creatures who have adapted to the city, like the blind fish and glowing eels that live in deep water. New Yorkers usually say they could not live anywhere else. But I wondered what Oliver would say about the chattering Afghan taxi-driver or the hurrying wild-eyed Lubavitscher snatching at his side curls, or the slumped-over man selling gum in the rain. There were always people talking seriously and loudly to themselves, uttering menaces. There were always people taking refuge in doorways, or doubled up with laughter – what's so funny? Or else they were hunkered down in front of shops muttering 'Blee-blee'. There were ranters, and people looking for trouble, people with tics and palsy, people who had been discharged years ago from hospitals and were 'decompensating'. Decompensating might mean howling in the street or taking a swing at passers-by, cackling in the subway car, or masturbating at passing traffic. There was nearly always someone looking desperate, lying in the doorway of Harry Winston Jewelers on Fifth, or squatting in the alcove of Sotheby's on Madison Avenue.

Dr Sacks liked the idea of street neurology, but it would have to be limited – his foot was bothering him. He said, 'I'd like to show you two people, one with Parkinson's and one with Tourette's. They are both artists.'

***

Oliver, very shy, is the man who has proven in his work that a person's so-called handicap often causes the development of new skills or the discovery of assets. He is far less emphatic about 'deficits'. He says there are compensations. There are sometimes greater compensations for the person who has an affliction – other skills, like the Andean villagers in H.G. Wells's story, 'The Country of the Blind' who understand everything, who miss nothing, precisely because they are blind. In that story it is the sighted man who is at a disadvantage.

He has known Ed Weinberger, a furniture designer, for 15 years. He has never written about him. As with many people in Oliver's life there is no clear distinction between friendship and treatment. It is a long-term relationship. The people are part of his life – perhaps the largest part of his life. Ed's story has taken many turns but it is still unfolding. Ed lives on the eighth floor of a building on the Upper West Side. When he answered the door he was canted over – he has Parkinson's. Oliver stepped aside and said almost nothing. It was what I had noticed at the hospital, a sort of group dynamic in which no one is a patient, no one in charge.

Oliver does not speak of cures; his genius lies in his understanding of patients, which draws on friendship and love and the long-term relationship.

Faced with a patient who has a severe neurological problem, he is open to anything: aromatherapy, music therapy, group therapy, acupuncture, hugging, hand-holding, fresh air, outings in the countryside – and of course even drugs, though as Oliver says, drugs often obscure the real cause of a problem and create misleading symptoms of their own. He wants to go beneath the symptoms to find the problem and treat it. Because this takes so much time, Oliver offers more hours to his patients than any other doctor I know, which perhaps explains why his medical earnings last year were $7,000 – a figure that was reduced to zero after he paid his malpractice insurance.

He is a listener of seismographic sensitivity, a clear-sighted and inspired observer, attentive, with an eloquence that allows him to describe a person's condition with nuance and subtlety. Oliver has said that his shyness – possibly caused by the wartime separations from his family – is a sort of disease. Shyness plays a part in his observation, giving him a vantage point, for shy people can be intensely watchful. It makes him patient. His patience and the tenacity of his observation make him the most compassionate and tolerant of men, with a capacity for seeing abilities where another doctor would see only deficits.

For the first half-hour or so at Ed's, Oliver hardly spoke. He did not want to intrude; he wanted me to form my own impressions. I soon saw that Ed's leaning was echoed in the furniture. In every table or chair, in desks and shelves, angles had been cut out of their surfaces, the corners were bisected, the legs seemed to lean and everything stood solid – the more solid for the way the angles supported them.

'Look at this.' It was a photograph of Ed crouched on a legless corner of a table that seemed to defy gravity.

Ed was a collector of well-made objects – old cameras and spy-glasses and telescopes, of Chinese jades and bronzes. He also had a vintage car, a 1948 Bristol, made in England.

'That's a lovely desk,' I said.

'I call it my "bridge desk".'

Arched like an eyebrow, it was an unusual wooden desk, of pale orange pear wood, sanded by hand, the details of grain matching the joinery very carefully, giving the illusion of lightness. The legs were splayed, somewhat like Ed's own.

The cantilever legs, he said, were based on a bridge designed by Robert Maillart. Maillart was a Swiss bridge engineer who revolutionised the designing of bridges, making them stronger and more slender, combining the whole – arch, girder and road – into one piece.

'And those angles I saw on the eye features of a Kwakiutl Indian ceremonial mask,' Ed said. 'The structural features of the mask interested me, especially the tension between the solidity and the surface.'

Many objects and pieces of furniture in the room looked as though they were about to topple over. Canted over himself, Ed said it was all a trick of the eye. He showed me a red desk with jutting planes and said that he had derived some of it from the Indian mask too. 'I wanted to give it the illusion of an extruded form.'

It was more solid and four-square than anything upright. He showed me the angle of the desk and said, 'Would you imagine this to be a 90-degree angle?'

It seemed to me much smaller, but placing a square

piece of cardboard in the angle, he showed me that it was absolutely square. It was important to him he said, that the angles in his work reflected the angles in his body and life. Needing his life to be angular he completely redesigned the furniture in his house and, in so doing, contrived to invent a totally new sort of furniture, a Parkinsonian-style, which was a way of standing and living. What another person might take to be an obstacle had given him a new conception of furniture.

Oliver then spoke for the first time. He said, 'It so reminds me of the person in *Awakenings* who says, "If only the world were composed of stairs, then I would be happy."'

'Before my operation, just a year ago, I began to think about buying a car and driving it,' Ed said.

The choice of car was interesting, Oliver said. He eventually acquired a Bristol, a vintage car which was characterised by an angular body. It was a substitute body – Ed would open the angular doors – with angles as interesting as the ones he designed for his furniture, angles as radical as his own posture – and he inhabited this body.

'I drive around Central Park, on Sundays when there is no traffic,' Ed said.

'Ed's passionate about cars. My version of that, I suppose, are the motorbikes I used to ride – Norton's.'

Oliver said that when he was doing his residency at

UCLA, there was a quadriplegic woman who said she wanted to go for a ride with him. Oliver knew that the woman did not have long to live.

'I thought I would grant her this wish,' Oliver said, 'and so my friends helped me get her on the back of the bike. They wrapped her up, tied her firmly on the seat, and off we went. She loved it. We all rode together, about six or eight motorbikes – the quadriplegic woman on the back of mine.'

He smiled, remembering the incident, and he fidgeted as though he had dislodged conflicting memories.

'We returned to face an aghast and curious crowd,' he said, and seemed to see the crowd of astonished faces, the untying of the quadriplegic woman from the pillion seat. 'My whole residence was characterised by episodes like this. As far as the department was concerned, I was somewhere between an embarrassment and an ornament.'

The quadriplegic woman had loved being sprung from the hospital and had delighted in the sensation of racing down the road on the back of a motorcycle.

Already I was glad we were away from the hospital and just having lunch in a New York apartment. I would never have known this fact about Oliver's motorcycling if Ed had not prompted it. As for the puzzled response of Oliver's department, this was to be repeated later, when in 1991, Oliver was let go after 24 years' working at Bronx State –

the Bronx Psychiatric Center – whose unimpressed executive director was quoted in the *New York Times* (16 February 1991): 'Dr Sacks was not considered particularly unique here. I am not sure he complied with state regulations.'

At the mention of hospitals Ed described various horrific experiences he had had in hospitals about four years before, when, heavily sedated with Elavil, halcyon and codeine, he had had a severe nervous reaction and hallucinations. From being a patient with Parkinson's he was diagnosed as psychotic. It seemed so.

'I thought I was being attacked by terrorists. I thought I was being set up. There were many episodes. I had the fantasy that I was being persecuted.'

He had to be restrained by male nurses. He was treated as someone who was out of his mind. The doctors who were supposed to be taking care of him were merely sedating him, but the effect was alarming. 'I was really crazy. The food was a problem, too. If you have Parkinson's you have throat problems – it's hard to swallow. They gave me rough food, not soft food. That could have choked me. I said, "You should give me soft food" – but they paid no attention. I spat it out. They thought that was very amusing.'

One day he overheard them saying that, although his condition was pretty bad, they wanted to go on giving him this dangerous medication in order to finish their experiment. This enraged Ed. He told them they were irresponsible. This had little effect.

'Then I called my own neurologist and told him to get me out of there, or I would sue them. That's what did it. The next day I was out of the hospital.

'One shudders to think how much this may go on. There was a woman who ran from Brookhaven, who then began to live among the fields and hedgerows of Long Island. They said, "She has discharged herself, against medical advice." You can't spend years – or even days – in a mental hospital and being treated as mad without it doing something terrible to you.'

Ed at home was easier to diagnose than Ed in a hospital. I said, 'So hospitals can be dangerous?'

'I come across many people who have been in hospitals for 20 or 30 years because of being misdiagnosed,' Oliver said. It was the old horror from 'Ward Number 6'. 'These so-called designer drugs – designer heroin. There are forms of it that render people profoundly Parkinsonian. Deaf people are mistakenly diagnosed as retarded. Post-encephalitics are sometimes locked up in mental hospitals as schizophrenics.'

Ed said, 'The doctor who was in charge of me was only interested in his work. To him I was just a body. It was like a prison camp. It was all ruthless indifference.

Sometimes, in order to be treated properly in a hospital you have to act crazy.'

An operation called a pallidotomy had saved him. He had opted for the operation because of the terror of hospitalisation and the severe Parkinson's which at times had given him episodes – some as many as six hours long – of utter immobility, being stuck in one rigid posture in which he had been unable to move. But the operation had been risky. It was brain surgery that involved targeting a very precise area in the brain and destroying this. There are risks of intellectual and speech impairment due to the location of the target area. The procedure worked – Ed was liberated. Before the operation he had been immobile: could not walk, could not talk, could not get up from his chair.

'I have been reborn,' Ed said. 'I have a new life.'

It seemed to me that Oliver's friendship and insight was as essential to Ed's understanding as the surgeon's knife. Ed's ambition was to fly to England, pick up a new Bristol – the angular car for the angular man – and drive to Switzerland, to look at the gravity-defying angles of Maillart's bridges.

**

Street neurology, Oliver said, allowed 'the spur and play of every impulse'. The true test of this was perhaps accompanying a very ticcy Touretter (Oliver prefers this word to Tourettic) through New York. Shane F., who is mentioned in passing (another splendid footnote) in *An Anthropologist on Mars*, happened to be visiting New York from Toronto, and so Oliver suggested that the three of us go to the Natural History Museum. In Shane, Oliver said, 'I would see Tourette's as a disease. As a mode of being. As a mode of inquiry.'

When we met Shane in front of the hotel on 81st Street, he rushed to Oliver, hugged him, touched his face and became excited, vocalising an urgent and eloquent grunt, 'Euh! Euh!' as he described a motor accident he had just witnessed.

'But some people came up to help!' he said in his hurried stuttery way, like a child trying to discharge a whole thought and stumped by syntax in the excitement.

He went on describing it, and from that first moment he dominated us. Also from that moment Oliver seemed to withdraw. He was a presence, no more than that, sometimes a shadow, sometimes a voice, always a friend, and often his figure – protective, supportive and yet entirely unintrusive – was that of an ideal parent.

Shane was 34 but seemed younger because of his explosive gestures and great energy and eagerness. He had black hair and bright eyes; he was handsome and vital, humorous and talkative, too impatient in his inquisitive chattering to wait for an answer. He did an imitation of President Clinton, then one of Oliver. He said, 'I can't drive but I was driving Oliver's car! Euh! Euh! Oliver was saying, "Do pull over, Shane. Just pull over." And I was driving. Not too fast, but fast! "Do pull over."'

He caught the Englishness and the slight stammer in Oliver's voice.

And this was also the first indication I had that when Shane was mimicking someone's voice or accent he was so concentrated he ceased to be Tourettic.

We got into Oliver's Lexus (the air-conditioner preset at 65 degrees), and headed off to look for a parking place. Oliver had two large plastic cuttlefish on his dashboard. One fell off and, in righting it, Oliver swerved and Shane cackled. Oliver was disoriented, he took several wrong turns, and none of us had any idea where we might park. And so for 15 or 20 minutes, while Oliver murmured, narrating his mistakes in driving, Shane was talking, gesticulating, ignoring the search for a parking place and talking excitedly.

'Oliver's writing about Pingelap and Pohnpei – did he tell you? Or is he too shy? He was writing about the achromatopes – Euh! Euh! He went there – Euh! – twice. Toronto's my town, but you know the people are more aggressive in my city than they are here. Euh! I find people

110

a lot friendlier here. I prefer New York. I like the frenetic strange – euh! Oliver is Mister Mushroom-Maniac.'

'Not really, but I love lichens,' Oliver said, and then, 'Just put it in a lot,' still narrating his movements at the wheel, and parked it.

Leaping out of the car, Shane ran around to Oliver again and hugged him, touched his face, grunted, stamped the heels of his boots. Oliver just smiled – it was like father and son – and Oliver said, 'Yes, yes, well...'

As soon as we crossed the street, Shane took off, without even grunting in farewell. He shot down the sidewalk, sprinting towards the Natural History Museum like a Bushman through tall grass, very fast, his arms pumping.

'Imagine Shane in space,' Oliver said, watching him with pride.

'One violent movement and he would push the shuttle off-course.' Oliver smiled at the thought of a space-capsule jerked out of orbit by the Tourettic astronaut inside. Several times Oliver mentioned with genuine amusement the possibility of highly sophisticated technology upset or destroyed by such tics or flailings.

Seventy-eighth Street seemed the perfect place for a Touretter. Shane smelled a light-pole, and then gripped it and swung around it. He moved on, touching posts, stooping to touch the kerbstone, the sidewalk, the parking meters. Then he sniffed the parking meters. He rushed back. He touched both my elbows, then Oliver's, dashed on ahead again, and found some more parking meters to sniff, and ran on. Now I knew why the heels of his boots were so worn.

'Why does he touch those posts?'

Oliver was implacable. 'Ask him,' he said.

Shane smiled to my question. He said, 'You're looking for a rational reason. Euh! Euh! But if I told you, would you believe me? Would you think I was telling you the truth? I touch them because they're down there, this one and then that one.' He twisted his head and grunted again.

'Is the reason I gave you the right reason?'

Soon he was moving too fast for me to keep up with him and persist in my questions. Oliver just smiled.

On this June afternoon, a cool day after days of heat, people were strolling but few of them noticed Shane. This was New York City. Shane did not seem unusual; he did not stand out in the crowd. He waited for the 'Walk' sign, he jeered at the bad drivers, the honkers, the speeders, and when the light changed and we walked across Columbus Avenue, Shane was running, stopping to touch the low stone walls of the museum, or the gate-posts, or the trees. Now and then he hugged a tree, and sniffed it, pressing his face against it.

'He remembers everything,' Oliver says. 'Everything he touches. Everything he smells.'

He seemed to me like someone making a new map of the city, his very own map, on which every object had a unique shape, and temperature, and smell and texture. In his Manhattan, every parking meter was different. There was no such thing as 'a parking meter'. There was only, say, 'The sixth parking meter on the north side of West 78th Street, east of Columbus Avenue', like Funes in the Borges story 'Funes the Memorious' who can't understand why the word 'dog' stands for so many shapes and forms of the animal, and more than that, 'it bothered him that the dog at three fourteen (seen from the side) should have the same name as the dog at three fifteen (seen from the front)...'

Shane ran onward, calling out, 'Hup! Hup! Hup!' A white dog on a leash sensed Shane's hurrying, became agitated and leaped into its mistress's lap. This interested me, because no one else paid much attention, but the dog reacted to him as though to another creature – not as a threat but as something large and alive with whom it would have to share its space. The dog began barking – not at Shane but in a generally upset and distracted way, alarmed and excited. Shane laughed, and replied with his own 'Euh! Euh!' because he had sensed the dog too.

Apart from that, Shane was lost in the crowd. Odd and ticcy as his behaviour was, it was not more extraordinary than that of the gigglers and shouters, the roller-bladers, the youths with hats on backwards and carrying boom-boxes, the woman pushing a supermarket trolley crammed with plastic bags, the two haggard men sharing a bottle wrapped in brown paper, the screeching girls, the murmuring old men, the snuffling man raggedly dressed as a cowboy. Now and then someone smiled at Shane – no more than that, a smile as a shy query. Only the little white dog was truly alarmed; and the woman who owned the mutt was more alarmed by the dog, as it skittered on her skinny thighs.

So far, in terms of street neurology, it seemed that a world-class Tourettic was just about invisible on a New York sidewalk except to a small dog.

'Sometimes Shane creates misunderstandings,' Oliver said. 'And occasionally they are serious misunderstandings. But usually it is no worse than this.'

We entered the Natural History Museum. I bought the tickets, Shane barked and coughed and chattered, and he smelled the turnstile as he went through it.

Running ahead, Shane loudly read the signs – all the signs: 'It says you can't cross this... "Danger Man-eating Plants"...You know this type of tree...Look, there's a little chipmunk in this...I didn't know they go underground... "Winter is a period of inactivity"... Euh! Euh! Babies over here... You see what's buried under there? It's a food cache... Nuts. Nuts.'

He touched and pinched Oliver, he touched walls and doorways, he ran his fingers over plaques, he moved rapidly from one exhibit to the other. He drew a long breath and seemed to inhale everything he saw. Then he said, 'Let's sit down and take a good look,' as though willing himself to be still.

We sat in front of the scene of rural winter, a cross-section of the countryside. Dead leaves on the ground, mulch below that, rodent tunnels and rotting vegetation.

'Tree roots remind me of the brain, for some reason,' Shane said.

'Yes, dendrites,' Oliver said. 'So they can make maximum contact.'

'Look at that decay,' Shane said. 'It looks like what goes on inside my refrigerator.' The sight of decay launched Shane into a frenzied description of the movie *Soylent Green* – his favourite, he said – its prophetic visions of a dying planet: ozone depletion and dead oceans and over-population. This explanation calmed him a little, and he finished by saying that he wanted to see the tigers. We found three stuffed tigers in a glass-fronted exhibit.

Knowing that Shane is an artist, and judging from some of the paintings Oliver had shown me, a very good artist, I said, 'What do you see?'

'This is meant to inspire nobody. It doesn't inspire fear

or awe. This is a base comparison to the real thing. Euh! Euh! This is a mausoleum-like glass enclosure, sort of pathetic. It's like a memory, the ghost of a ghost. There is no reality to this. It doesn't make sense. Why don't they stuff humans and put them in here? You know, the tiger in life can stand very still. A tiger can stand breathless and frozen. As Oliver would say,' and here he slipped into Oliver's donnish accent again, '"It's Parkinsonian... It's... it's lithic..."' But these tigers have only the shape and the memory but not the lithe movements. In other words, a sculpture could better this. They're not infused with life.'

'What do you think of the tigers in the zoo?' Oliver asked. I wondered whether he asked it because of Shane's love of tigers and his own tigerish movements, his leaping and pouncing.

'They're in cramped quarters, and they're depressed and even regressed. One we saw had a pacing behaviour. But you know the two-edged sword is that the zoo is meant to protect them.'

'But do you have any sense of Blakean wonder at the zoo?' Oliver asked.

'Yeah, I did, Euh! Euh! – because it was a living tiger. But I don't know – it's a captive. A captive in your imagination. You can never really capture a tiger. I'd like to have an exhibition of my tiger paintings.'

Shane hurried on to the room signposted Invertebrates, and Oliver paused, smiling gently, making a note on a small pad. We moved on to Giant Invertebrates.

'I love the gelatinous,' he said. 'I love the cephalopods.'

A Giant Squid (*Architeuthis princeps*), 50ft long, dangled from the ceiling. Oliver smiled at it. Shane was walking quickly in circles among the exhibits of squid, touching benches, smelling signs. He moved purposefully, his head up, his hair damp with perspiration.

'I met someone the other day who had been bitten by an octopus,' Oliver said. 'The octopus is very intelligent. One was being examined in a tank. In another tank an octopus was watching.' He glanced at Shane, who was sniffing and touching, and said, 'It makes you wonder whether parts of the brain die because they aren't fed and stimulated.'

'Brains, brains, euh! Aarrgh!' Shane was hugging Oliver again.

'We used to eat brains all the time,' Oliver said, as Shane poked at him. 'I remember my mother serving it – sheep brains – and cutting the cerebellum. "There's the dentic nucleus, Oliver. Eat it."' He smiled.

'What about your family, Shane?'

'My father's Jewish. My mother's crazy.' He tapped my notepad. 'Put down Canadian.' He began pacing again.

A thin, leathery-faced Indian man approached Oliver.

He woggled his head and said, 'I heard you speak in Rotterdam.'

'Yes?' Oliver said.

The Indian said, 'Do you remember my question?'

Oliver stepped backward and took a better look at the man.

The Indian said, 'About Tourette's. Can it manifest itself at an elderly age?'

'Oh, yes,' Oliver said. 'But I can't remember what I told you. Not long ago, I met a woman who was 58. Her Tourette's manifested when she was 52. So it is possible.'

'Oliver, Oliver, Oliver, Oliver,' Shane was chanting, and he was grunting too. He was calling Oliver's attention to a pair of dinosaur skeletons, an Allosaurus attacking a long-necked diplodoccus. Shane then began to imitate the movements of each creature – the leaping Allosaurus, the roaring Diplodoccus.

Nearby, a man was making a charcoal sketch of the Allosaurus on a large drawing-pad – the pad was four feet by three feet. Some people were sitting on benches, lovers were holding hands, kids were squalling. Shane paced up and down, making dinosaur faces, dinosaur gestures. He approached the man sketching and began commenting on the man's picture. The man listened. Shane asked for a piece of paper. Without a murmur, the man tore off a large piece for Shane.

'Newsprint,' Shane said, and twitched violently. 'It's not good quality.'

With a mixture of charm and chutzpah, and uttering sudden sounds, he put his hand out. I thought the man was going to hit him. The man gave him a piece of charcoal. Shane threw the piece of paper on to the floor, and crouched on it, poised like the attacking Allosaurus and began sketching rapidly.

Oliver had been pacing, not impatiently, merely it seemed to get some sort of perspective. I approached him. He said, 'I have never seen him do this before.'

Oliver slipped away. I drifted over to Shane as, I suppose, Oliver thought I might. The next time I looked up I saw that Oliver was looking at Shane and me. In pursuit of street neurology I had believed that I would be observing Oliver, and of course I had, to an extent. But Oliver was elusive; he evaded my glance, he stepped out of sight, or stayed firmly in the background. He listened, he let others talk, and only when they were done did he put his oar in.

Some people gathered to watch Shane swiping at his sketch, ignoring the man who was slowly scraping away on his pad. In minutes, Shane was done.

'The gesture, the gesture, see? Hup! Hup!' Shane said. 'The whole movement, euh!'

Shane dropped the picture and began pacing rapidly

again, vocalising, as he had been throughout the making of his sketch. I picked up the sketch and brought it over to Oliver.

Oliver said, 'One wonders to what extent these highly gifted people's imaginations may be flavoured by the gesture – the movement. It immediately seizes and is seized. Some of Shane's pictures are of animals in motion. But there are also some highly symbolic ones, about starvation, exile, torture.'

Shane's picture was amazing, for its speed of execution and its accuracy. It was the Allosaurus in motion, and even the other artist approved, and so did the passers-by. Shane was skipping around the room, touching the walls, smelling the pillars, tapping the benches. From time to time he would return to Oliver, as though to a reference point, touching his arms and shoulders, and hugging him. Oliver simply smiled.

We left the museum. Shane sprinted, Hup! Hup! Hup! and vaulted a planter by a doorway. He called to Oliver, 'You do it!'

Oliver said in a self-mocking Edward Lear-like way, 'I am an elderly gentleman and can't be expected to do that.'

Shane was not listening. He was headed down the sidewalk, his arms pumping – Hup! Hup! Hup! He touched the posts of an awning. He drummed his fingers on a kerbstone. He saw a bench – he sat on it quickly and just as quickly leaped up, saying, 'Euh! Euh!'

Seeing him, a woman rushed to her baby carriage and with a quick-step that spoke of alarm she hurried away, thrusting the carriage in front of her, away from Shane.

I said, 'Why did that woman leave in such a hurry?'

'She was frightened,' Shane said.

'Why do you suppose she was frightened by you?'

'I'm a man.'

'So she's afraid of men?'

'She saw a man moving. That maybe bothers her. She's nervous. She's got a little kid with her.'

'Why should she be worried about you?'

'This is New York.'

***

We went to a café. Oliver seemed baffled by the menu. He stammered and then decided on tea. Shane ordered tea, too, but talked so energetically he did not drink it. He talked about Robin Williams, Lenny Bruce, ecology, deforestation, floods, dumping raw waste ('Bizarre plumbing practices'), tourists, Aids in Thailand, the Galapagos, Victorian science and coprolalia.

'Sometimes in Tourette's there's coprolalia – compulsive swearing. I don't have coprolalia, except sometimes, when I'm alone,' Shane said. 'When I'm painting, then sometimes I swear. All the words, ahem! Euh! Lenny

Bruce's performances were attacked and he was prosecuted for his obscene language. He was told to modify it or fuck off. There are so many ironies – the police themselves use that language in the police station.'

Oliver said, 'You swear less than most policemen.'

'I swear when I have touching tics. I touch my bed. My comments usually involve my family.'

'In the eight years I've known you I really haven't heard this,' Oliver said. 'Only ten or 15 per cent of Tourettes patients have it. Some people have severe motor tics but no coprolalia. The only identical behaviour I've found has been in Tourettic twins, in Atlanta. They both have elaborate erotic phantasmagoric behaviour, such as calling out the window, "My father's raping me!" Or there was a time at the beach when they shouted, "Shark! Clear the beach!"'

'I did that!' Shane said. He was rising. He was fidgeting again. Out of the café he sprinted ahead and began talking loudly, chattering to people on the sidewalk. I tried to catch up with him, but I was weary – nothing was more fatiguing than an outing with a Tourettic. But he was still bright. A young woman smiled at him. She was about 23 or 24, in cut-off jeans and a blue patterned bandana.

'Hi, hi, hi,' Shane said.

'I know you,' the woman said. 'You're famous, aren't you?'

Shane was vocalising – barking and coughing. He touched her elbow very gently. She took his hand and they started down the sidewalk together, holding hands. Shane then sprinted with her, hurrying her forward. As though energised by him the woman laughed excitedly.

Behind me, Oliver said, 'The car's up here,' and pointed in the opposite direction.

Seeing Oliver standing so calmly, I saw again, as I had seen in the museum, that he was helping me get to know the process of approaching neuro-history by setting up such a meeting. But the encounter between Shane and the woman served him, too, by offering him contrasts, and different points of view. In Oliver's view, human behaviour is prismatic, multi-layered, and his life and his work have proved that revelations come over time. In this natural neurology, treatments in the fourth dimension, personality is not painted in primary colours but shown rather in a million subtler hues, delicately shaded, and even as Oliver has written in another context as 'a polyphony of brightnesses'. A solitary person is monochromatic. When others are present, the personality is suffused with colour.

I remembered something that Oliver had said about a man at Beth Abraham whom a hasty doctor might term a vegetable. Oliver had spent decades treating the man. True, the man was confined to a wheelchair but – the phrase stayed with me – 'He is emotionally complete.'

Oliver was looking past me, in the direction Shane had taken.

'I'll get him,' I said. But I could not see Shane.

Shane and the young woman had gone two blocks before I caught up with them. It was only because of their being blocked by traffic that I caught them at all. Shane could easily have hurried the woman away. She looked as though she wanted to be hurried away.

To this young, fresh-faced New Yorker, Shane was not a Tourette's sufferer, nor ticcy, nor gesticulating wildly, nor hurrying up and down in an inexplicable manner. He was another New Yorker, an energetic young man, talking fast and stammering and grunting. He wore a black jacket and cowboy boots. Had the young woman looked, she would have seen that in an afternoon of sprinting through streets and museum corridors the heels of the boots had been worn flat. One person had been frightened by Shane – the woman with the baby. A few people had smiled at him. Most had not noticed him. Only the dog had been spooked.

This young woman was madly attracted, and she scowled at me when I approached and spoke to Shane.

'We have to go,' I said. 'Oliver's way down there, waiting for us.'

'Shane, who's this guy?' After a two-block sprint she was already on a first-name basis with him.

'I have to go,' Shane said. 'Dr Oliver Sacks. Down there! Euh! Euh! Give me your number – I'll give you a call.'

'If you blow in my ear,' she said and screeched with pleasure.

Shane blew lightly into her ear as she wrote her name and her telephone number on Shane's Natural History Museum brochure.

'Do it more! Oh, that's nice!' Then she hugged him. 'Call me Baby-Doll.'

'Euh! Euh! Baby-Doll.'

'I love you!' she said, and kissed him.

Shane smiled at her. He had made a friend – he could easily have spent the night with her. I stood watching with my arms hanging down. Then Shane was off, sprinting again. I started after him, but he surged ahead, dodging people on the sidewalk, and leaped across the street, ahead of the traffic. He got to Oliver before the light changed, the nimblest pedestrian in New York, leaving me on the wrong side of the street, but both of them watching me.

I understood then, that at the hospitals, with his friends, in the street, and now at the end of the day, it had always been part of his intention to observe me, and more, to see the interplay between the person and me – the aphasic, the choreac, the paranoid, the Parkinsonian, the Touretter, even the colleague and the close friend. I was not an observer, and this was not an interview but part of his life and the psychodrama of a New York outing, street neurology in the widest sense.

AUTHOR BIOGRAPHY

Paul Theroux's many novels include The Mosquito Coast *and*
Picture Palace, *which won the Whitbread Prize for Fiction. His
travel books include* The Great Railway Bazaar *and* The Pillars
of Hercules. *In 1998 he published* Sir Vidia's Shadow, *a memoir
of his friendship with Sir Vidia Naipaul. His latest novel,* Hotel
Honolulu, *was published by Hamish Hamilton in April 2001.*

Other books in the **FRONTLINES** series:

British Teeth
An excruciating journey from the dentist's chair to the
rotten heart of a nation
William Leith

The Strange World of Thomas Harris
Inside the mind of the creator of Hannibal Lecter
David Sexton

Funeral Wars
How lawyer Willie Gary turned a petty dispute about
coffins into a multi-million-dollar morality play
Jonathan Harr

Last Drink to LA
Cleaning up on the West Coast of America:
confessions of an AA survivor
John Sutherland

Your Pedigree Chum
Like most dog-lovers, Missy's owners think she is irreplaceable –
and they are rich enough to do something about it
James Langton